CONTENTS

D0570287

YEAR
OF
THE
SURV

Outplay. Outwit. Outlast. They survived, variously, a desert-island game show, a quintuple bypass, Olympic competition, a Cuban-American family feud and a bitterly contested election. Toughing it out (from left): Richard Hatch, George W. Bush, David Letterman, Cathy Freeman, Al Gore, Susan Hawk, Elián González and Rulon Gardner.

Here's the freshman class of Survivors, just before the games began on Pulau Tiga, their island home in the South China Sea. Seated, from left: Gervase Peterson, Jenna Lewis, Joel Klug, Stacey Stillman, Greg Buis, Colleen Haskell. Standing: Ramona Gray, Dirk Been, Gretchen Cordy, Richard Hatch, Sonja Christopher (distinguished for being the first voted off), Susan Hawk, Kelly Wiglesworth, Sean Kenniff, B.B. Andersen and Rudy Boesc

One Is the Loneliest Number

Gilligan meets *Lord of the Flies* on TV's most addictive hit

Eating beetle larvae or eluding sea snakes wasn't the most amazing feat performed by the intrepid debut cast of *Survivor*. No, what was most impressive was that for four months after leaving the South Pacific taping site, the 16 castaways and 140-person crew resisted the media bulldogs and kept the winner a secret. (Okay, maybe it wasn't that hard: All involved had signed a contract making them liable for $4 million if they squealed.) In addition to the voyeuristic appeal of watching 16 strangers in bathing suits (or less) attempting to befriend one another even as they strive to come out on top, that secrecy was key to the show's popularity. Each week,

20 million viewers tuned in to see who would be voted off the island—no recounts allowed—and the finale outrated every 2000 show except for the Super Bowl.

Would former Navy SEAL Rudy Boesch, 72, beat out the 22-year-old rafting guide Kelly Wiglesworth? Was the alliance between straight-talking truck driver Sue Hawk, 38, and conniving corporate trainer Richard Hatch, 39, based on trust or strategy? America also tuned in for moments like homophobic Rudy slathering sunblock on the openly gay Rich. Or the sweet and polite student Colleen Haskell, 23, finally telling Rich off: "Go home and go get your liposuction and go catch

more fish, 'cause you're bugging me." Looking back, perhaps we could have seen it coming. Rich was the star of nearly every scenario, from the battle over the right to join Sean Kenniff, 29, for a luxe breakfast off-island (after eating nothing but fish, rice and rat for weeks) or his own birthday celebration, in which Rich strode the beach in his birthday suit. At the final tribal council, Sue indicted two-faced Kelly as a rat, and venomous Rich as a snake. On Pulau Tiga, snakes trump rats. So, too, in their game. When Jeff Probst, the island's clean-cut Mr. Roarke, held up his name on the tiebreaking ballot, Rich Hatch was the only one who looked surprised.

"The homosexual," said homophobic retired Navy officer Rudy Boesch (right) of openly gay teammate Richard Hatch, "he's one of the nicest guys I ever met."

Host Jeff Probst lodged with the rest of the crew in a cushier compound of buildings on the far side of the isle.

Gervase Peterson, 30, a basketball coach, got squeamish and lost his team's second immunity challenge—eating beetle larvae (inset, above). In the appetizer course the bugs were deep-fried, and almost palatable. In the second round of play they were raw and wriggly and oozed brown goo when bitten.

Cameras, along with sand fleas and stingrays, swarmed the castaways. After the show ended, producer Mark Burnett revealed in a behind-the-scenes book that the crew had rooted for Gretchen to win, and that Greg, the staff's least favorite, was by far the most odoriferous player.

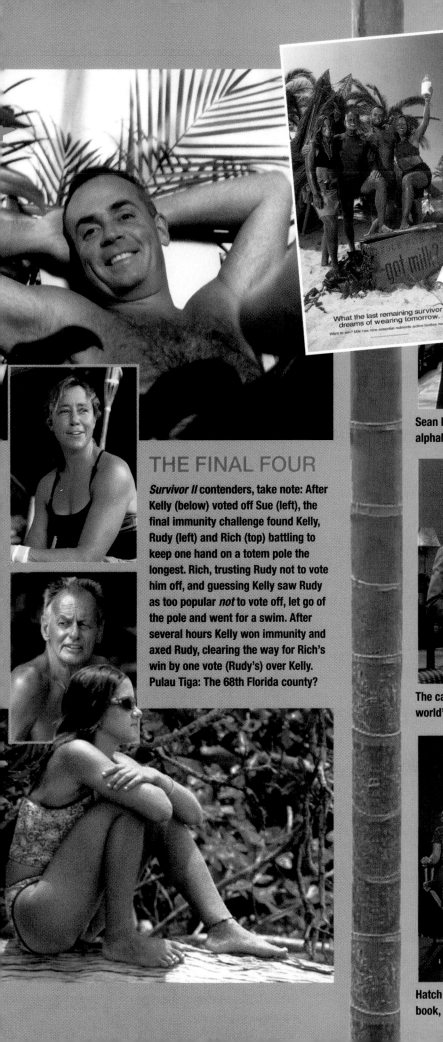

ENJOYING THEIR 15 MINUTES

Only one got the million. But nearly all cashed in on their hard-won fame. Many, who now have agents, sat in on *Hollywood Squares*. Colleen shot a movie. The final four (left) shilled for milk.

What the last remaining survivor dreams of wearing tomorrow.

Want to win? Milk has nine essential nutrients active bodies need.

Sean Kenniff, the neurologist who voted off cast members alphabetically, landed a TV-news doctor job in New York City.

THE FINAL FOUR

Survivor II contenders, take note: After Kelly (below) voted off Sue (left), the final immunity challenge found Kelly, Rudy (left) and Rich (top) battling to keep one hand on a totem pole the longest. Rich, trusting Rudy not to vote him off, and guessing Kelly saw Rudy as too popular *not* to vote off, let go of the pole and went for a swim. After several hours Kelly won immunity and axed Rudy, clearing the way for Rich's win by one vote (Rudy's) over Kelly. Pulau Tiga: The 68th Florida county?

The candidate, the monochromatic *Millionaire* host and the world's most famous trucker met on *Live with Regis Philbin*.

Hatch (center, in black), the first also to come out with a book, vamped with his castmates on *Letterman*.

Dubya Moves into Poppy's Old House

After an angry endgame of demonstrations, dueling lawyers and way too many late-night 'pregnant chad' punch lines, Texas governor George W. Bush follows in his father's footsteps

Bush (speaking in Wisconsin) joked that the best campaign advice had come from his wife, Laura, 54, who told him, "Don't try to be charming, witty, or debonair. Just be yourself."

Dimpled chad? Judge Charles Burton, Palm Beach canvassing board chair, eyes a ballot. Theresa LePore (left), designer of the butterfly, lost 18 pounds in the aftermath.

"You ain't seen nothing yet!" said Gore (in California). By November 8 his words had become prophetic. But his scramble for votes in the Florida courts and counting rooms fell short.

Last fall, Bush's twin girls Barbara (left) and Jenna became freshmen at Yale and the University of Texas, respectively.

"Listen, son," said Bush Sr. (in Austin with Laura, W. and Barbara, awaiting returns) early on. "I love you whether you run; I love you whether you don't run."

Weeks after the election, the world was still wearily awaiting a winner. Voters did, however, have a pretty good idea who the 43rd President of the United States would be. However the dimples were decreed, the victor would be a political scion, raised at the knee of a Washington insider. He would be a Southerner educated in New England's Ivy League. He would enjoy enough baby boomer credibility to talk not only about having inhaled but also about the importance of affordable prescription drugs for an aging population. And he would go down in history as having won his country's highest office in the most bitterly contested election of modern times.

From the moment they cinched their nominations relatively early in the primaries, it was neck-and-neck for Vice President Al Gore, 52, son of a U.S. senator from Tennessee, and Texas governor George W. Bush, 54, son of the former President. Rarely did the front-runner

du jour ever lead by more than the statistical margin of error. Gore kissed his wife and pulled ahead. Bush kissed Oprah and got a bounce.

Indeed, both candidates' families served as more than photo-op props. Exuberant Tipper Gore, 52, helped humanize her comically stiff husband. A garage rock drummer as a girl growing up in Virginia, she became an outspoken crusader against obscene rock lyrics. More recently, she championed the mentally ill. She herself had recovered from clinical depression after their son Albert III nearly died when hit by a car in 1989. The Gores' two oldest daughters spoke at the convention, and the charismatic Karenna translated the pop culture to the wonky, seemingly tin-eared old man. Sibs Sarah, 21, and Albert, now 18, kept lower profiles, as did the Bush twins.

Jenna and Barbara, 18, mostly just followed Dad's progress from

their college dorms. Laura Bush, 54, a former librarian raised in Midland, Texas, and the bookish member of the household, shied from the press more than her Democratic counterpart, but offered W. good advice: It was her idea that he go on *Oprah*.

Without a decisive issue such as Bill Clinton's "It's the economy, stupid" strategy, which helped oust Bush père from office in 1992, each candidate struggled to find a theme. Bush, projecting an approachable, just-folks image, maintained it was all about character, while Gore, with 24 years in government versus Bush's 6, insisted it was about experience and expertise. At the beginning, at least, personal attacks were limited, and the second debate patty-caked into a lovefest. Bush tripped over his tangled tongue ("I know how hard it is to put food on your family," he earnestly told low-income voters), Gore on his penchant for embroidered tales (a labor song he claimed his mother sang as a lullaby wasn't written until Al was 27).

Their running mate choices did speak volumes. By tapping Sen. Joe Lieberman, 58, one of the most vocal Democratic critics of Clinton during the impeachment, Gore blared his "I am my own man" message. Bush, taking the opposite tack, added his father's well-seasoned former Secretary of Defense, Dick Cheney, 59, to his ticket. Lieberman was the first Jew on a national slate, and Bush had made a point of featuring nonwhites at the convention, including the family of brother Jeb, the Florida governor, whose

wife, Columba, is Mexican.

As weeks passed and neither campaign found leverage, the quipping turned nasty. Wags cracked that the Republicans' idea of diversity was topping the ticket with executives

from two different oil companies. The Gore team used Bush's mostly innocent misstatements as evidence that he was simply too dim for the job: Did the governor really not know that Social Security was a federal program? Meanwhile, the Bush camp stopped kidding about Gore's purported claim that he invented the Internet (actually a misquote) and instead tried to draw parallels between his exaggerations and the far more egregious misstatements of the Clinton era.

Two flavorful third-party candidates also vied for votes. Pat Buchanan's hard-right, anti-trade populist attack proved a negligible factor except in what turned out to be

Reporters (above) teased Bush with masks and shirts that referenced his inadvertently miked slur of a *New York Times* writer. Left: "This guy doesn't like somebody in his face. I'm going to get in his personal space," said Gore, who did, during the third debate.

The day after the election, Gore made a show of relaxed confidence by staging a Kennedyesque family football game (with son Albert).

Daughters Karenna, 27, a recent law school grad, and Kristin, 23, a TV comedy writer, stumped for Dad on *The Tonight Show*.

At the convention, Gore and Lieberman each touched on policy issues from gun control to the environment. Their stand on, er, public bussing was a crowd pleaser.

Florida's pivotal Palm Beach County, where a confusing butterfly ballot gave him votes meant for Gore. The Green Party's Ralph Nader, 66, landed about an equal 2 percent of the total vote but with more seismic impact (see box, right).

Come election night, the TV and scrambling new cable networks' race to declare a winner from exit polls led to an embarrassing miscall of Florida—first for Gore and, hours later, for Bush. Shortly after, Gore phoned Bush to concede. Then, after most of the country had gone to bed and the Florida tally again drifted back into the uncertain column, Gore rang back to retract. When Bush protested that Jeb had assured him he had carried Florida, Gore countered, "Let me explain it to you. Your younger brother is not the ultimate authority on this."

Bush was, in fact, certified the Florida winner, but by a small enough margin to trigger an automatic machine recount. Democrats, emboldened by Gore's upset and a 300,000-ballot win in the national popular vote, demanded a hand recount, and world-class lawyers and spin doctors soon flooded the state. Protesters took to the streets (some of them practiced from the earlier González rallies), and the war went all the way to the Supreme Court. A fed-up nation knew that although it would eventually have a new President, people would need convincing that the winner was truly presidential.

FROM FRINGE TO HINGE

Three advocates of campaign finance reform elevated the dialogue. A Vietnam hero, John McCain (below) seemed an antidote to what the GOP saw as the morally slippery Clinton regime. Refreshingly unscripted, the Arizona senator handily won the New Hampshire primary but was out of it by March, having been outspent 10-to-1 by Bush. Gore, meanwhile, easily routed the even more charisma-impaired ex-senator Bill Bradley in the Democratic race. Ralph Nader (above), the consumer crusader turned Green standard-bearer, declared a pox on both (by his lights) corporate-puppet parties, sluicing away votes mostly from Gore, including some 97,000 in Florida.

Though she campaigned for Bush, and sits in his brother Jeb's cabinet, Florida secretary of state Katherine Harris, 43, maintained that she could be objective overseeing the recounts there.

Ups Down Under

Athleticism triumphed over drug-use issues and schmaltzy, taped TV

While 10,200 of the world's finest athletes competed in a record number of events at the tape-delayed Sydney Games, U.S. viewers perfected three skills: (1) ignoring the suspense-killing, real-time results (hardly easy: A Visa ad congratulated California's Stacy Dragila before her pole-vault victory had aired), (2) keeping a thumb poised over the remote to mute the swell of music signaling another sappy bio feature, or (3) just tuning out (ratings were the lowest since 1968).

Those who hung in were rewarded with a plethora of powerful moments. The North and South Korean teams marched together in the opening ceremonies. The underpopulated host country collected 58 medals (fourth behind the first-place U.S.'s 97); five of them went to the "Thorpedo," swimmer Ian Thorpe. And there was, of course, the Cinderella hero, an unlikely Greco-Roman wrestler from Wyoming (page 19). "Overall, it was a successful Games," declared track ace Marion Jones, who coolly took five medals back to L.A. despite the distraction of having her husband, C.J. Hunter, a shot-putter sidelined with injuries, charged with steroid use. The Olympians proved far more compelling competitors than the Survivors who aired opposite them in reruns. While U.S. audiences may have cursed Romania for capturing the women's gymnastics, their sportsmanship prevailed in sympathy for Andreea Raducan, who forfeited her gold after testing positive for a drug contained in a cold pill she'd taken. Controversy couldn't mar the "no worries, mate" atmosphere: Sydney closed the Games with a parade of 200 drag queens.

Venus Williams (left), 20, took the singles tennis gold and shared the doubles crown with her sister. But Serena, 19, collected 100-plus souvenir pins of the nations, more than any other jock in the Olympic Village.

In a cascade of water, Cathy Freeman, 27, lit the cauldron to open the Games, uplifting her Aboriginal people and inspiring her Australian teammates to 16 golds, including her own in the 400-meter run.

Lenny Krazelburg, 24, trained by the Soviet sports machine until emigrating to L.A. in '89, won two backstroke golds and a third in the medley relay.

Despite three prelim-game losses, the U.S. softballers rallied for the gold. 'Twas the second for Dr. Dot Richardson (below), 39, who may now hang it up.

His Aussie coach said if he were to build a swimmer, his Frankenstein would be Ian Thorpe, 17, starting obviously with the size-17 flipper feet.

No one but the world's fastest woman, Marion Jones, 25, would be disappointed to get only three gold and two bronze medals.

Sydney 2000

THE MOST UNLIKELY WIN

Without the WWF costumes or that "Let's get ready to *rumbllllle . . .*" guy, it seemed a long shot that America would even tune in to Greco-Roman wrestling. But thanks to the 12-hour tape delay and NBC hype, the nation was tipped off to the biggest upset of the games when Rulon Gardner, 29, raised on an Afton, Wyoming, dairy farm (inset), snatched the gold from Alexander Karelin, 33, the Russian champ who hadn't lost a match since 1987. Did you get that? The last time Karelin was defeated, George W. Bush's dad hadn't been elected yet. That Gardner won surprised even himself. "I didn't think I could," said the self-described "goober farm boy," and he celebrated by cartwheeling his 286-pound frame on the mat.

GOT RULON?

The youngest of eight, Rulon "got more than his share" of chores on the family farm, said brother Russell (standing, second from right).

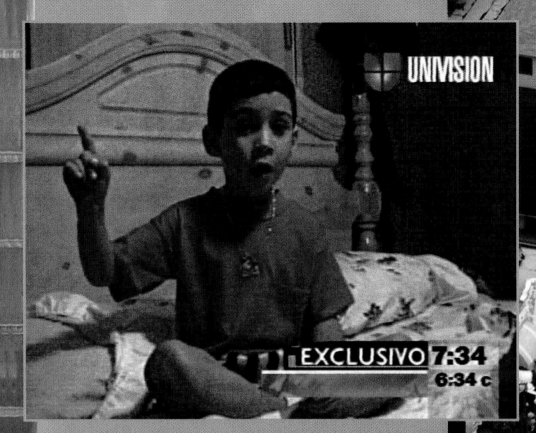

EXCLUSIVO 7:34 6:34c

UNIVISION

The Long Journey Home

After seven months of living in a nation divided over who should raise him, Elián González returns to Cuba

In April, when Elián González's father arrived in the U.S. to claim his son, his Florida relatives hoped that he might grow to love the country as his 6-year-old had. Just as Elián adored Pokémon, chocolate milk and Disney World, they counted on Juan Miguel finding joy in the freedom and abundance of America. Yet Juan Miguel wanted only his son, and to return to Cuba. His Miami kinfolk resisted, but U.S. immigration authorities supported the dad's right to decide. "We tried every way we could to encourage [Juan Miguel's uncle] Lázaro González to voluntarily hand over the child," said Attorney General Janet Reno, who had acted as a mediator. "[They] rejected our efforts, leaving us no option but the enforcement action." On the morning before Easter, armed federal agents raided Lázaro's home and plucked Elián from the arms of the fisherman who had rescued the boy last year, and had since moved into the family fold. An AP photographer captured the moment, giving critics fodder to portray Reno's America as more oppressive than even Castro's Cuba. Soon a powerful competing image hit the wires: that of a little boy smiling in the arms of a loving father. The Miami relatives filed another suit to keep Elián in the States, but lost on final appeal in the U.S. Supreme Court. In June, Juan Miguel and Elián, wearing a Pokémon pendant, flew home to Cuba, where the boy is now a second grader.

"Papa, I don't want to go to Cuba," said Elián in a videotape (left, above) made by his relatives in Miami. "If you want, stay here." Were these the wishes of a 6-year-old, or words scripted by his great-uncle? Protesting Cuban-Americans thought it was the former, and pressed for Elián's asylum.

"What do I have to do to prove that I love my child?" asked Elián's dad, Juan Miguel González, wearing a T-shirt with his son's image before their reunion in Washington.

Because his mother died while trying to give Elián freedom, many Cuban-Americans (forming a human chain around the González home) felt the U.S. should honor her goal.

At sea in 1999, Elián witnessed the drowning of his mother, Elisabet Brotons (with the boy in 1996). He spent two days adrift on an inner tube before being pulled in on Thanksgiving Day.

Marisleysis González, 21, acted as a mom to her cousin while he was in Miami. She reported that during the seige, agents had threatened, "Give me the boy or we're going to shoot."

By September, Elián had blended in with his uniformed classmates in Cárdenas and was no longer a poster boy for refugee rights or a Cuban national icon.

After a court turned down the last appeal by the Miami relatives, Juan Miguel González was free to take Elián home. On June 28 they boarded a charter plane from Washington, D.C., to Havana.

Fisherman Donato Dalrymple tried to hide Elián during the raid. Later that day the boy played with a toy plane as he flew to meet his dad.

RAZOR'S EDGE

Decades ago their clunky wheels ruled the sidewalks; then they disappeared like dinosaurs. Now scooters are back with a vengeance—sleeker, lighter, faster, pricier. The reborn scooter entranced both adults and children in 2000. The Razor brand was rolled into America from Taiwan by Carlton Calvin, an attorney who founded Razor USA in California. At $99 for two Rollerblade wheels and a collapsible metal frame, Razors proved an instant hit. Soon the young and the young at heart were pumping their way to work or play. By November, Americans had snapped up an estimated 7 to 8 million scooters of various brands. Then motorized versions (right) joined the buzz. Emergency rooms buzzed too: From January to August, more than 9,400 riders wobbled in with injuries (nearly 9 out of 10 were kids under 15). Now helmets and pads are proliferating. Carlton doesn't sweat consumer backlash. "It's still pretty restrained," he says. "Compared to Pokémon."

This is my better half.

KEEP IT PUM...

KEEP IT PUM...

Who Knew He Had a Heart?

After a bypass, David Letterman suffers his pals' loving barbs

In 18 years of late-night television, David Letterman, 52, had never taken a sick day. But after a routine angiogram in January found a clogged artery, the wise-cracking host suddenly required a quintuple bypass. He joked with the nurses ("What? I came in for *cosmetic* surgery!") but also took his condition seriously: A heart attack had killed his father at age 57. The procedure left the Letterman heart "as sound as a 20-year-old's," said cardiothoracic surgeon O. Wayne Isom, who had also treated Larry King and Walter Cronkite. And after five

weeks of rest, Letterman returned to a reduced schedule, with pals like Bill Cosby and Kathie Lee Gifford (who made the crack in this story's headline) taking up the slack. Sideman Paul Shaffer said, "I knew everything would be all right" when on the first night back Letterman did his customary pre-monologue toe-touch. Jerry Seinfeld stopped by to say, "I thought you were dead," but Dave's reentry ratings so buried rival Jay Leno that *Late Show* executive producer Rob Burnett suggested "another quintuple bypass for May sweeps."

Patch Adams? No, Robin Williams (in scrubs) was the first guest when the *Late Show* reopened for business. Also that night, Letterman, choking back tears, introduced his real doctors and nurses. Fans in a Manhattan office (left) cheered on their neighbor.

A SCARY MISTAKE

Dana Carvey thought it was a joke when he learned his surgeon had "bypassed the wrong artery." In 1998 he had undergone a double bypass to correct a life-threatening blockage. Two months later another MD caught the mistake. To ensure "that the surgeon would not hurt someone else, and acknowledge his error," Carvey sued and donated part of the damages to cardiac research. A repeat operation fixed the problem, relieved wife Paula (above) and their two sons and enabled Carvey, 45, to resume jogging and to pinchhit for recuperating buddy David Letterman.

A COMIC'S SICK HUMOR

Diagnosed with testicular cancer in March, Tom Green, 29, saw his illness as an opportunity for both education and comedy. Taping his surgery, and the days surrounding it spent with family and his fiancée, Drew Barrymore, 25, he turned MTV's *Tom Green Show* into a darkly funny and touchingly raw hour of TV. (The sing-along self-diagnosis was priceless.) Now cancer-free, he and Barrymore plan to wed in 2001.

PEOPLE'S PEOPLE

Making a list . . .

Checking it twice . . .

Time again to remember

who's pretty, who's sexy,

who dressed poorly, who nice.

Here, we present a gallery of

intriguers, beauties and others

who made 2000 memorable

PEOPLE'S 50 MOST BEAUTIFUL PEOPLE OF 2000

Ben Affleck, *27*
actor

Joshua Bell, *32*
violinist

Candice Bergen, *54*
actress

Billy Campbell, *40*
actor

Neve Campbell, *26*
actress

Nick Carter, *20*
singer

George Clooney, *39*
actor

Tom Cruise, *38*
actor

Penélope Cruz, *26*
actress

Alison Deans, *39*
financial analyst

Bo Derek, *43*
actress

CHARLIZE THERON

"I'm 50 percent farm girl," says the South African star of *The Legend of Bagger Vance.* "I can milk cows and get dirty and, when the time is right, put on heels and do my hair." In beauty, as in life, timing is everything.

MOST BEAUTIFUL

Kate Dillon, *26*
  model

Scott Erickson, *32*
  baseball player

Rupert Everett, *40*
  actor

Cristián de la Fuente, *26*
  actor

Jan-Michael Gambill, *22*
  tennis player

Galen Gering, *29*
  actor

Heather Graham, *30*
  actress

Faith Hill, *32*
  singer

Amy Holmes, *26*
  political commentator

Iman, *44*
  businesswoman

Ashley Judd, *32*
  actress

Ashton Kutcher, *22*
  actor

Michelle Kwan, *19*
  ice skater

Jude Law, *27*
  actor

Matt LeBlanc, *32*
  actor

Ananda Lewis, *26*
  veejay

Nia Long, *29*
  actress

Rob Lowe, *36*
  actor

Andie MacDowell, *42*
  actress

Ricky Martin, *28*
  singer

Dylan McDermott, *38*
  actor

Soledad O'Brien, *37*
  TV anchor

CATHERINE ZETA-JONES

Why not endorse cosmetics? asks the Welsh actress's dad. "You'd save millions." An admitted makeup junkie, Zeta-Jones graced *High Fidelity* this year and, she says, spent heavily on salves to combat stretch marks before the birth of her son with Michael Douglas, Dylan.

GEORGE CLOONEY

Though he's AWOL from *ER*, fans saw Clooney in a dramatic live telecast of *Fail-Safe*, which he also directed, and at the movies in *The Perfect Storm*. For the latter, the darkly handsome star went for a more grizzled look. "They'll say, 'He looks awful,'" predicted Clooney. Sure, George, whatever you say.

T-BOZ

A very pretty member of TLC, Tionne Watkins cowrote their No. 1 hit "Unpretty," in part "to teach kids that nobody's flawless." But her beau, rapper Mack 10, says, "I'm looking for a flaw, and I can't find one."

MOST BEAUTIFUL

Amanda Peet, *28*
  actress

Tracy Pollan, *39*
  actress

Freddie Prinze Jr., *24*
  actor

Rania, *29*
  Queen of Jordan

Julia Roberts, *32*
  actress

Brooke Shields, *35*
  actress

Henry Simmons, *29*
  actor

Hilary Swank, *25*
  actress

T-Boz, *30*
  singer

Charlize Theron, *24*
  actress

Ming Tsai, *36*
  chef

Tina Turner, *60*
  singer

Shania Twain, *34*
  singer

Blair Underwood, *35*
  actor

Goran Visnjic, *27*
  actor

Denzel Washington, *45*
  actor

Catherine Zeta-Jones, *30*
  actress

DREW BARRYMORE

Having spent 19 of her 25 years in the public eye, Drew Barrymore finally began to do some of her best work behind the scenes. As a producer, she signed on Cameron Diaz to *Charlie's Angels,* with this sales pitch: "It'll be a chick action movie. We get to be beautiful and tough and wear badass clothes." Soon she had herself, Diaz and third angel Lucy Liu kicking across screens in a major hit. A child star who confessed her drug addiction in a memoir at age 14, she is now grown-up enough to value a private life. Though not shy about smooching in public with her fiancé, comedian Tom Green, at the last minute she called off plans to wed him midbroadcast on *Saturday Night Live.*

MOST INTRIGUING

BEN STILLER

"Ben has a worried look even when he's being charming," said Jay Roach, who directed Stiller in *Meet the Parents.* "Ben was terrified of [costar Robert De Niro] up front," said Roach. If nothing else, Stiller had material to draw on: He got real-life in-laws marrying actress Christine Taylor, 29.

HILLARY CLINTON

First Lady had been a fitting title for Hillary Rodham Clinton: the first to use her maiden name in the White House, the first lawyer (and also the first subpoenaed to testify in her own defense before Congress). In January, she'll be the first to move from senior political spouse to junior senator, from her adopted state of New York.

THE ROCK

"Can you smell what the Rock is cooking?" he will bellow. It's Dwayne Johnson's way of saying, "Know what I mean?" Zillions of kids do. As the Rock, the 6'5", 275-pound former football player has slammed his way to the World Wrestling Foundation title, spoken at the 2000 Republican Convention and signed a $5.5 million movie deal. "I've been blessed," he has declared, "with a considerable amount of charisma." No argument from his wife of three years, Dany, a Merrill Lynch associate vice president.

BEST DRESSED
LESS—SOMETIMES A WHOLE
LOT LESS—IS MORE

Jennifer Aniston, *31, actress;* Pierce Brosnan, *48, actor;* George Clooney, *39, actor;* Samuel L. Jackson, *51, actor;* Heather Locklear, *39, actress;*
Freddie Prinze Jr., *24, actor;* Kevin Spacey, *41, actor;* Britney Spears, *18, singer;* Charlize Theron, *25, actress;* William, *18, prince*

HEATHER LOCKLEAR *sparkled in*
Loewe at the Golden Globes.

SAMUEL L. JACKSON *topped*
Armani with an ad for his movie.

LIL' KIM *got maximum exposure at the MTV Video Music Awards.*

JENNIFER LOVE HEWITT *blew it with skin, sequins and feathers.*

PORTIA de ROSSI *mismatched polka dots and python boots.*

WORST DRESSED

WE LOOK BACK AND ASK, "WHAT WERE THEY THINKING?"

Christina Aguilera, *19, singer;* Lara Flynn Boyle, *30, actress;* Jennifer Love Hewitt, *21, actress;* Lauren Holly, *36, actress;* Lil' Kim, *26, rapper;* Lucy Liu, *31, actress;* Bebe Neuwirth, *41, actress;* Portia de Rossi, *27, actress;* Bruce Willis, *45, actor;* Renée Zellweger, *31, actress*

SEXIEST MEN

CASPER VAN DIEN

In high school, "they called me 'Ken Doll,'" recalled Sexiest Soap Star Casper Van Dien of the new nighttime serial *Titans*. "I wanted to be G.I. Joe, not Ken." Whichever, he wound up attracting ex-*Dynasty* vixen Catherine Oxenberg, 39, as his wife.

RUDY BOESCH

Boesch, though a runner-up on the summer TV hit, took first place as the sexiest survivor—to the total disbelief of his old Navy SEAL buddies. "He has an aura," says pal Billy Burbank. "Us guys don't see it, but the women sure do."

HEATH LEDGER

Appearing in a Mel Gibson film isn't necessarily the best way for a prospective sex symbol to get noticed, but fellow Aussie Ledger turned heads as Gibson's son in *The Patriot*. Among them: his new girlfriend, Heather Graham.

BRAD PITT

In the year 2000, commitment is sexy. So sexy, in fact, that Pitt, who wed Jennifer Aniston in July, is PEOPLE's first two-time Sexiest Man Alive. But that doesn't mean a girl can't dream. "He's drop-dead gorgeous," coos country singer Patty Loveless. "He has the greatest lips. I know he's married, but I just love him."

SEXIEST MEN AWESOME AUSSIES

Russell Crowe, *36, actor;* Adam Garcia, *27, actor/dancer;* Mel Gibson, *44, actor;* Darren Hayes, *28, pop star;* Lleyton Hewitt, *19, tennis player;* Steve Irwin, *38, wildlife expert;* Hugh Jackman, *32, actor;* Heath Ledger, *21, actor;* Costas Mandylor, *36, actor;* Julian McMahon, *32, actor;* Guy Pearce, *33, actor;* Mark Philippoussis, *24, tennis player;* Patrick Rafter, *27, tennis player;* Ian Thorpe, *18, swimmer;* Keith Urban, *33, country singer*

10 WONDER WOMEN

VANESSA WILLIAMS

Salsa dancing and Pilates was the antidote to the 40 pounds she put on with each of her four pregnancies. Though pleased with the results, husband Rick Fox of the L.A. Lakers says he's most attracted to "her selflessness."

MICHELLE PFEIFFER

She's "every bit as beautiful without any artifice as when she's lit and carefully photographed," raves *What Lies Beneath* costar Harrison Ford. But that beauty will be a scarcer commodity, as the mom of two (and wife of TV virtuoso David E. Kelley) plans to devote more time to family.

SELA WARD

A mother for the first time at 37, and again at 41, Ward maintains her spectacular shape by balancing the seesaw, she says, between the StairMaster and Krispy Kreme doughnuts. "I wouldn't turn back the clock," insists the *Once and Again* star. "I'm happier and more confident now than I've ever been."

39

RED-HOT GRANDMAS

SUZANNE SOMERS

Maybe there was something to those ThighMasters after all. Folks "gasp," Somers reports, when they hear she has five grandchildren. "I love it!" But, she frets, "when they stop gasping, I'll know I finally look like a grandmother."

JOAN COLLINS

A grandma for the first time at 65, Joan Collins couldn't get used to the title. So granddaughter Miel (now 2) was taught to call Collins "Dodo," a nickname the actress originally had as a child.

MICHELLE PHILLIPS

Phillips's first grandkid is the child of her daughter Chynna and son-in-law Billy Baldwin. "I'm sure it's surreal to see your daughter holding her own daughter," observes Chynna. "This whole grandma thing has been a little shocking."

The Most Public Parkinson's Patient Quits His Day Job

"That last night we felt like a great family," said Michael Boatman (below, far right) of Fox's final taping in April. During the fall season the cast (right, celebrating the wrap of their 100th episode) welcomed a new press secretary, played by Charlie Sheen.

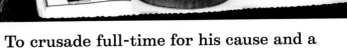

To crusade full-time for his cause and a cure, Michael J. Fox hit the final *Spin* cycle

"How can you argue with his decision?" asked *Spin City* mayor Barry Bostwick. "If I had Parkinson's, would I be as generous in protecting my fellow workers? Or would I crawl into a hole and feel sorry for myself? When you have a finite amount of energy during the day, you want to be where the love is." For Michael J. Fox, 38, that meant giving up playing press secretary Mike Flaherty to spend more time with his wife, Tracy Pollan, 39, and their kids, and to dedicate himself to fighting Parkinson's disease, from which he has suffered since 1991. For much of his four years on the show, he hid his condition and restructured his medication schedule to tame his muscle tremors during the weekly tapings. "That [meant] in the morning, he [might] be in pain," said castmate Alan Ruck.

Though Fox went public with his diagnosis in November 1998, it wasn't until a vacation in January 2000 that he decided to quit. "I feel that my time and energy would be better spent with my family and working toward a cure," he said. "I didn't suddenly take a turn. [The disease] hasn't debilitated me. I feel good and I'm happy, and there's stuff to do." At the top of his list was starting a Parkinson's foundation, an informational Web site (michaeljfox.com) and testifying before a Senate committee to boost research funding. His appearance netted an increase of $10 million but fell short of the $75 million he, and scientists, had urged. Fox will still act occasionally, he says, and continue as a *Spin City* executive producer. But his days will no longer revolve around a fictitious city hall. They will be spent playing with his twin daughters Aquinnah and Schuyler, 5, and son Sam, 11. And with Pollan, whom he thanked lovingly in his third Golden Globe acceptance speech. But he clearly hadn't retired his comic timing when he added, "Actor out of work. Film at 11."

Children of Misfortune

The killing of Kayla Rolland by a fellow 6-year-old shocked America anew

The day before he shot her, Kayla Rolland's 6-year-old killer had tried to kiss the little girl, his classmate in a Michigan elementary school. It had seemed like an ordinary exchange. "One minute they're fighting, the next they're hugging," noted prosecutor Arthur Busch of young children. The following morning the boy said to Kayla, "I don't like you." She faced him and replied, "So?" Then he took out a .32-caliber handgun and fired a bullet into her. Paramedics tried unsuccessfully to revive the girl as the young gunman cowered in the boys' room. Thirteen children had died in a dozen such school incidents in the past three years. But this one seemed particularly horrifying. The shooter had gotten the gun in a crack house where he lived with an uncle after his mother was evicted from their home (his father was in jail for violating parole after a drug possession). "He was basically living in hell," said Sheriff Robert Pickerell. Legally too young to form criminal intent, the child was not charged. The onus, instead, was on the 19-year-old who owned the firearm, and he was sentenced to 15 years. Small comfort for Kayla's mother and stepfather, Veronica and Michael McQueen, or for parents who knew it could have been their child. Said one mourner: "This isn't just a family tragedy."

Neighbors gathered in a vigil outside the elementary school to remember Kayla (left, bottom). Such shootings, said President Clinton, "have shaken our entire nation."

The killer's mother, Tamarla Owens (center), said her son apologized for his crime. Still, it is hard to know if he understood it. At the police station, he quietly drew pictures.

MOMS' DAY AT THE MALL

"There are those who say, 'Have a gun for protection.' I know better," said Courtney Love, mom to Frances Bean, 8, and the widow of Kurt Cobain, who died of a self-inflicted gunshot wound. Hundreds of thousands of mothers and others (including Athena Bradley and daughter Katie, right, from New Jersey) hit the capital to demand gun-control legislation—including trigger locks and background checks at gun shows—that the NRA and most Republicans in Congress opposed. The turnout "far exceeded our expectations," said organizer Donna Dees-Thomases. Said marcher and mother Susan Sarandon: "If we can regulate driving a car, we can regulate owning guns."

V

A Long, Brutal Summer

In the West, thousands battled heroically against one of nature's worst infernos

When a combustible mix—hot weather, dry lightning storms, high winds and forests made dense by the El Niño climate shift—coalesced to create the worst wildfire season in 50 years, the most elite units of America's bravest mobilized in the Northwest to try to contain it. "The first day we got here," observed Jim Tomaselli (a California fireman assigned in Montana), "we worked a 39-hour shift." Some firefighters lost as much as 25 pounds in the course of the summer despite constant gorging on sweets and energy snacks.

More than 26,000 men and women—members of the Park Service, the Forest Service and the armed forces—were deployed in 12 states threatened by the fires. "Thank You, Firefighters," read signs crafted by those grateful for their help, even as hundreds of families were forced to evacuate their homes and make snap decisions about what few possessions to carry with them. Despite the heroic battle against some 74,000 separate fires, more than 6.4 million acres—an area bigger than

Vermont—were lost by August, and relief would not come until the rains of October. With reinforcements flown in from Canada and Australia, the operation cost as much as $18 million per day.

The intrepid crews arrived in the Northwest haunted by a recent disaster in New Mexico. In May at Bandelier National Monument, the Park Service had set a controlled "backfire," intending to prevent a bigger one, which the winds inadvertently whipped into an unmanageable holocaust. That blaze burned out a total of 50,000 acres, destroyed 400 homes, uprooted 20,000 people and threatened a Los Alamos laboratory housing a stockpile of plutonium and radioactive waste. Admitted Secretary of the Interior Bruce Babbitt: "The calculations that went into this were seriously flawed." Only when it was finally contained did Battalion Chief Juan Pacheco allow himself to "break down and cry." He thought back and recalled feeling "sorry for the people who lost everything" and being "thankful that no one got hurt."

"You're constantly thinking of all the things that could go wrong," said Karen Scholl, 31, the sole woman on the 20-person Del Rosa Hot Shot team from San Bernadino, California. She passed along orders to Dan Adams, 27, who thought positive: "We're paid to go hiking and camping."

The roar of fire consuming whole acres at a time (in Thompson Creek, Montana, left) sounded like a freight train, reported George Custer of the Southern Fire Management team. "Mother Nature," he marveled, "is amazing."

Love Under Fire

Hip-hop's It Couple of Jennifer Lopez and Puffy Combs survive a tough year

"It's not like Cinderella meets the Incredible Hulk," said music writer Sacha Jenkins of Jennifer Lopez and Sean "Puffy" Combs, both 30. "They have a lot in common." Both grew up in low-income New York City neighborhoods—she in the Bronx, he in Harlem. And both parlayed talent and astonishing drive into early success. In less than a decade she went from a dancing "Fly Girl" on TV's *In Living Color* to a platinum-selling pop star and actress commanding $5 million a picture. A business major at Howard University, he founded Bad Boy Records, which took in over $54 million in 1998. They also have in common one horrible night that left some wondering if Lopez, clearly smitten with Combs, couldn't do better. While at a Manhattan nightclub in late 1999, a protégé of Combs, rapper Shyne, allegedly fired a gun, wounding three people. After fleeing the scene with Lopez, Combs was charged with illegal possession of a different gun, and with attempting to bribe a witness in the case. His trial will begin in 2001. The indictment was announced the day of the Grammy Awards, when he was up for best group rap performance and she for best dance recording. But Combs seemed to have his mind, like the rest of the world, on his girl and her down-to-there dress (see page 72).

A Real Quickie Marriage

**Setting a new low in high-concept TV,
two strangers wed before 23 million viewers**

"It took something like this to make the Miss America Pageant look good to me," said National Organization for Women president Patricia Ireland of FOX TV's matrimonial game show *Who Wants to Marry a Multi-Millionaire?* The premise: 50 women would compete by answering *Dating Game*–style questions and parading in swimsuits to win a proposal from an unseen rich dude. (FOX provided the 3-carat diamond ring.) Los Angeles nurse Darva Conger, 34, who claimed to have appeared on the show only to get the trip to Las Vegas, where it was taped, was the big winner. Or loser—it was hard to tell at first. On the air, she smooched new husband Rick Rockwell, 43, a San Diego comic/real estate agent worth about $2 million but called by friends

"incredibly cheap." A week later, with the cameras off, Conger demanded the annulment that the show's producers had promised to all contestants. "We're not two people who could ever get along in real life," she said after returning from a Caribbean cruise "honeymoon" during which she and Rockwell lodged in separate cabins and were accompanied by a chaperone. At the same time, one of Rockwell's ex-girlfriends revealed that she had taken out a restraining order against him after he had broken into her home and hit her—charges disputed by Rockwell. Conger, meanwhile, set about convincing the nation that she was not a publicity-seeking gold digger and was, in fact, a private person. She did so, in part, by appearing nude in *Playboy*.

Slavs to Milosevic: Time for You to Go

Vojislav Kostunica's election ends a 13-year reign of terror in Yugoslavia

Among his first promises as Yugoslavia's newly elected leader was a refusal to live in the presidential palace. "I will never move to somebody else's house," said legal scholar Vojislav Kostunica after unseating the unpopular but politically dominant Slobodan Milosevic with 53 percent of the vote, an event historians called "miraculous." Kostunica, 56, will rule from the small apartment he shares with his wife, Zorica Radovic, 56, and their dog and two cats. His populist approach came as a welcome change to a country weary of Milosevic's egomaniacal warmongering and corruption. Though Kostunica (pronounced kohsh-TOO'-nee-tzuh) opposes the NATO presence in Yugoslavia, his win was praised by the U.S. and European Union, which lifted sanctions against Serbia in response to the ouster of the man responsible for ethnic cleansing campaigns in Bosnia and Kosovo. Kostunica had won two weeks earlier, but Milosevic refused to acknowledge he had been voted out. Then throngs of angry voters stormed the Parliament building in Belgrade to help convince him by wielding torches and shouting, "He is finished!" Finally, when Kostunica was allowed to address the crowds and his country as their chosen leader, he began simply, "Good evening, dear liberated Serbia."

An 11-year-old neighbor of Kostunica (above, just after his swearing in) said, "He's very nice, always says hi." The young constituent asked if the new president might outlaw school entrance exams.

After two weeks of uncertainty, citizens of Belgrade (left) cheered the end of Yugoslavia's Milosevic era, which saw war, economic ruin and political isolation.

At a prison 50 miles outside Belgrade (right), rioting inmates demanded better conditions. On the roof, some held aloft a banner reading, "Long Live Kostunica."

The Accused

Wen Ho Lee leaves prison after a wrongful rush to judgment

"I haven't seen the moon for nine months," marveled Dr. Wen Ho Lee, at home in White Rock, New Mexico, after 278 days in near solitary confinement. Charged in 1999 with 59 counts of espionage, Lee was accused of sharing U.S. nuclear secrets with the Chinese government. Denied bail, the 60-year-old Los Alamos laboratory researcher was considered such a threat to national security that he was shackled whenever he left his cell.

At the start of the inquiry 20 months earlier, Lee hadn't worried about being questioned, because, he told his family, he had done nothing wrong. But his daughter Alberta Lee, 26, thought they should hire a lawyer. "I told her she'd been seeing too many movies," said her brother Chung, 28. But her instincts proved correct when an FBI agent likened Lee's alleged actions to those of Julius and Ethel Rosenberg, convicted of spying for the Soviet Union and executed in 1953. Alberta put on hold her career as a technical writer to aid in her dad's defense, enlisting the press and the support of Asian-Americans to make public the racial aspect of the allegations. By August the government's case had fallen apart as evidence could not be produced, and one FBI agent said he had testified falsely. Accepting a plea bargain, Lee did admit to one count of transferring, for reasons unexplained, more than 400,000 pages of classified files to a nonsecure computer. A judge sentenced him to time served, and apologized for governmental conduct that had, he said, "embarrassed our entire nation."

A heat-seeking missile, Eminem performed in Montreal, appeared in a Michigan court on gun charges and (inset) saw wife Kim in better days.

Eminem's Day in Court
The subject of his bilious rap wants a divorce

"The relationship is not great," says Eminem's manager Paul Rosenberg, of the rapper and his wife, Kim. "I mean, he writes songs about killing her." Eminem, born Marshall Mathers III, became rap's preeminent white star by composing such inflammatory rhymes. That the couple, who wed in 1999 after a decade of dating, filed for divorce surprised no one. In June police arrested Eminem, 28, for allegedly attacking a bouncer he believed his wife had kissed. Onstage he told fans, "You might have heard something about me and my wife having marital problems. But all is good between [us]. In fact, she's here tonight." Then he pulled out an inflatable "Kim" doll, simulated sex acts with it, and tossed it to the crowd. In July, Kim attempted suicide; she wound up hospitalized with minor razor cuts. "It was a cry for help," said her mother. Help may arrive with the divorce. But first will come a custody battle over their daughter Hailie, 5, and for the $10 million Kim is seeking for "intentional infliction of emotional distress."

COME IN, HOUSTON

She was supposed to sing at a tribute to Arista Records chief Clive Davis. She didn't. She was supposed to be at the Oscars. Faith Hill filled in, leaving everyone asking again, Where's Whitney Houston? Before the Grammys, where she dedicated a win to hubby Bobby Brown, her last high-profile appearance had been in a Hawaiian airport, where she was charged with toting 15 grams of marijuana. Perhaps Houston, 37, was hiding from rumors: of drug use or of a pending breakup. (She has denied both.) In May, Brown, 33, was jailed for violating his DUI probation and spent 65 days behind bars. Upon his release in July (below), she leaped into his arms.

A Legal Victory for Love

Vermont's legislature gives same-sex couples all the rights of marriage

Prior to a historic ruling by the state supreme court, Vermont's most influential pair was Ben & Jerry. But last year the court decreed that Nina Beck and Stacy Jolles were entitled to the same "common benefits" as heterosexual couples, even if they could not legally marry. Beck, 44, a physical therapist, and Jolles, 41, a psychologist, had applied in 1997 for a marriage license and were turned away. Beck (above, holding son Seth, with, clockwise, fellow plaintiffs Jolles, Lois Farnham, Peter Harrigan, Stan Baker and Holly Puterbaugh) says she is "very excited" at the prospect of not only a wedding but also the more important rights that come with marriage: insurance coverage, medical decisions,

family-leave benefits, among others. In its decision the Vermont court directed the state legislature to either legalize gay marriage or to create a legal status for same-sex domestic partnership. In the spring a bill passed that reaffirmed the definition of marriage as being between one man and one woman but permits gay and lesbian couples to register in civil unions and enjoy the same legal marital perks as other spouses. In reaction to the landmark Vermont law, 30 states passed "Defense of Marriage Acts," which deny the legitimacy of same-sex unions. "People will see," retorted the Lambda Legal Defense Fund, "that the sky has not fallen in Vermont when families are respected this way."

The Doctor Is In (Hot Water)

On-air provocateur Laura Schlessinger offends with her biological theories

Four years ago Laura Schlessinger, possessing only a Ph.D. in physiology, set up shop as a self-help expert on radio. Her mandate, she proclaimed, was to bring the world "wit, wisdom and no whining." And though she had not spoken to her own mother in years, she blithely offered up parenting advice and soon accrued 18 million daily listeners, making her the most popular host in the genre. That popularity suffered in 2000, however, when Dr. Laura declared that homosexuality is a "biological error," gays are "sexual deviants," and homosexual men are "predatory on young boys." Paramount, her syndicator, somehow ignored the controversy and launched a TV version of her program.

But when protesters established Web sites like StopDrLaura.com, the studio started getting the message. "If someone referred to Jewish people as 'biological errors,' they would never have a talk show at Paramount," asserted Washington, D.C., lawyer John Aravosis, who helped register the Web site. Schlessinger countered that those who flooded Paramount with e-mails were "fascists." Prominent gay voices like Ellen Degeneres weighed in, denouncing Dr. Laura's wide reach as "dangerous." Bill Bradley, a presidential candidate at the time, said her statements made him "sick to my stomach." Still others acknowledged that she had a right to free speech, even if that speech made them cringe. "I don't believe in shutting anybody up," said singer Melissa Etheridge. Though Schlessinger never wavered from her position, which, she said, is rooted in the Bible, she did later allow that "some of the words I've used have hurt some people, and I'm sorry for that." Meanwhile, her fledgling TV show was banished to predawn time slots in many U.S. markets and faced extinction.

GROWING PAINS

LeAnn Rimes's father didn't just raise a daughter; he raised a star, shuttling her to talent contests from age 6. Promoting the young country singer was a family effort, but it was her big-as-the-sky voice that made *Blue,* her debut album, a bestseller and Grammy winner. For his work as manager, Wilbur Rimes, 47, paid himself (and a partner) an $8 million salary—a more than 30 percent cut. LeAnn earned only $5 million herself. Now 18, Rimes decided that was askew, and sued her father for $7 million. They settled quietly out of court. "My dad and I butted heads because he was, like, my dad trying to be my business partner," she said, conciliatorily. "In the end it all worked out. It was nice having him and my mom both around when I was 14, 15, 16."

Carnie's Conquest

A Wilson Phillips vet has lifesaving surgery

"I started to gain weight when I was around 4," recalled Carnie Wilson, now 32. "One reason was I didn't feel love from my father." Her dad, Brian Wilson, the formative Beach Boy, left the family when Carnie was 11. By the time she, her sister Wendy and their pal Chynna Phillips formed the pop act Wilson Phillips, she weighed 200 pounds. Still, she said, "I never felt inferior to or not as pretty as Wendy or Chynna, just not as svelte. Onstage, I never thought about it." But after the band broke up in 1992, she was forced to. When she hit 300 pounds and had trouble getting out of her car, doctors told her that morbid obesity (defined as being at least 100 pounds overweight) could lead to diabetes, heart disease or cancer. She opted for gastric-bypass surgery, which left her stomach, said Dr. Alan Wittgrove, the size of "a thumb." To inform others about the procedure, she allowed the operation to be broadcast over the Internet. Soon after, the weight began to drop off. Eight months after surgery she had lost 112 pounds. And two months later, her dad, with whom she has reconciled, walked her down the aisle at her wedding to musician Rob Bonfiglio, 32. He had fallen in love with Carnie at her peak weight, presurgery.

Wilson (above, in 1993, and below, in April 2000) went on the Web to explain the problem of morbid obesity. "People think, 'Oh, you're just fat and lazy.' It's a disease that's not taken seriously."

There to Share
Napster fights to keep its freedom

The computer code for Napster was written in under three months by 18-year-old college dropout Shawn Fanning, who aimed only to satisfy his and others' appetites for sharing free music. Just over a year later Napster (named for its creator's high school nickname—he had unruly hair) claimed 38 million users, making it the fastest growing Internet application in history. But small wonder: Napster allowed music lovers to swap song files with one another as easily as copying a CD to tape. It was free, fast and, alleged the Record Industry Association of America in a suit filed in July, illegal. Representing five giant media companies, the RIAA charged that Fanning's company committed "the largest mass copyright infringement in history." A separate supporting suit made unlikely allies of Metallica drummer Lars Ulrich and rapper Dr. Dre. The Web site is "trafficking in stolen goods," complained Ulrich. (Fanning, left, strutted at the MTV music awards, in a Metallica T-shirt he claimed to have borrowed from a friend.) Other musicians backed Napster, including Courtney Love, who argued that the software is "creating more demand for music." And in November, Napster struck a deal with Bertelsmann AG to revamp the site in order to track and pay royalties to artists whose music it copies. Bertelsmann then withdrew from the RIAA suit. Napster will probably have to charge fees to users. Fanning (by now endowed with $15 million of venture capital but no revenue) wasn't sweating Napster's fate, declaring, "I have a lot more ideas."

ALAS, SEEING LED TO BELIEVING

In a computer-generated image, Christopher Reeve, 47, paralyzed since a 1995 riding accident, appeared to walk again in a TV spot for an investment firm aired during the 2000 Super Bowl. The next day many families of similarly injured people, believing Reeve had been cured, called spinal cord groups about the seeming breakthrough. It was not the response Reeve had wanted. He felt the ad would be "a motivating vision of something that can actually happen." The actor also lent his image to a disability insurance company which, in lieu of compensation, gave $3 million to the Christopher Reeve Paralysis Foundation.

The Codebreaker

Craig Venter leads in the genome race

Biologist J. Craig Venter, 53, wanted the world to know he was first. That his company, Celera Genomics, beat by five years the National Institutes of Health's target for mapping the human genome—the genetic code for the stuff that makes people people. After sorting out the 3.1 billion biochemical "letters" that comprise the genome, Celera announced its discovery in March. Reading the genome will lead to clearer understanding of many diseases and may eventually help to cure them. Spurred on by Celera's pace over the last 10 years, the NIH said it would release its version just a few months later. Given the significance of the development, Venter (left) and the NIH were encouraged by the government to share credit for a milestone comparable in scope, say scientists, to the first moon landing. But neither Venter, who believed Celera should own the rights to the information, nor Francis Collins, 50, the biologist who heads the NIH project and saw Venter's approach as unscrupulous, could agree how that would work. "Fix it," President Clinton ordered his science adviser. "Make these guys work together." In June they did, issuing a joint statement of shared credit. Now comes the hard part. Having laid out the map, both labs must set about learning what it all means.

Silver and Gold

Six years after his daughter medaled at the Olympics, Dan Kerrigan is a winner too

When figure skater Nancy Kerrigan won silver at the 1994 Winter Games in Lillehammer, Norway, it was a victory for her whole working-class family back in Massachusetts. Her dad, Dan, 60, had put in long hours as a welder and at odd jobs to support his brood of three kids, not to mention Nancy's expensive training. His wife, Brenda, who is legally blind, always minded the children at home. An inveterate lottery player, Dan won $20 on a scratch card in August and reinvested part of the earnings in three more tickets. One of them beat the game's 3.24-million-to-one odds and returned a clean million. "That's what happens when you get old," jokes Brenda. "You get a lot of practice at things. And he has had an awful lot of practice scratching tickets, I found out." At the time, Nancy, whose 3-year-old, Matthew, was home with Grandma, was touring Germany with husband Jerry Solomon. Her reaction? "No way! Are you joking?" Now her parents hope to enjoy some of the world travel that Nancy's pro skating career has afforded her. "I planned on retiring within a year and a half," says Dan Kerrigan. "This makes it much easier."

Luck Is a Lady Named Jay

A one-armed bandit hands a Vegas waitress a $35 million tip

It wasn't the costume or the cacophony of the casino that bothered Cynthia Jay, 37, about working as a cocktail waitress. It was seeing winners all around her, then finding how grudging were their gratuities. "I've gotten a bus token for a tip before," lamented Jay. "Sometimes you wish people would say 'Thank you,' that's all."

As a gambler, Jay normally kept to a $21 limit herself, either out of superstition, or practicality, given her $30,000-per-year earnings. But one night in January she went a little crazy. During an evening out with her boyfriend and his folks, she exceeded her cutoff and popped another three dollars into a Megabucks slot with odds of 50 million to one. On her ninth spin, the bells and whistles and sirens tolled for Jay: She'd won a $35 million prize—a new Nevada record. She resolved first to split the jackpot with her bartender beau, Terry Brennan, even though the couple had been dating for only eight months. After that, she says, she wanted to see that her family (she's one of eight kids) was "all taken care of." Then she would spend a little dough on herself, she figured, but added, "I still don't plan to be a different person." Though maybe a world-class tipper.

Jay (at the Desert Inn) surprised no one by announcing, "I really don't think I'll be going back to cocktails."

KNIGHT AND DAME, YOU ARE THE ONES

For years after completing his last James Bond flick, Sean Connery tried to shake the 007 moniker. And eight-time bride Elizabeth Taylor has certainly had trouble maintaining her "Mrs." status. This year both earned titles they will happily hold on to. Though they've toiled more years in Hollywood than in Britain, Connery and Taylor became Commanders of the Order of the British Empire. That is, he's now a knight, and she's a dame. Sir Sean, 69, who supports nationalist groups that seek the breakup of the empire, received his dubbing in his native Edinburgh, wearing Highland dress (above) and sporting, sources say, a concealed tattoo reading "Scotland Forever." The health-challenged Dame Elizabeth, 68, left behind her wheelchair to deliver a little bow to the Queen during her Buckingham Palace ceremony. "I can't believe it!" said Taylor, born in London to American parents. "I didn't think I was eligible." Later she celebrated with family and friends, including Michael Jackson (right). "We have already been instructed to refer to her at all times as Dame," said son Michael Wilding. Added Taylor: "If I'm not being referred to as That Broad."

"Thanks for Bringing Your Father," read signs welcoming Chelsea to India. In Jodhpur (right), she received a Hindu *tika*. Back in D.C. (below), she spent time with beau Jeremy Kane.

Doughnuts? Wasn't that Dad's thing? Chelsea and Candidate Clinton campaigned in Amherst, N.Y.

Chelsea Blossoms

With her mom seeking office, the First Daughter strode into a more public role

"You'll be seeing some of me," the poised young woman told a crowd of reporters outside New York's city hall. Wasn't it just yesterday that Chelsea Clinton was a 12-year-old brace face cheering her dad at the 1992 convention? Over the past eight years, as the press scrutinized her parents' political, financial and sexual lives, they have, for the most part, respected the younger Clinton's privacy. This year, with orthodonture and ballet recitals behind her, the Stanford junior sought out just enough media attention to aid her mom's run for a U.S. Senate seat. No word on whether she'll follow her folks into politics, though she did hint that she's interested in attending Oxford, where her father once studied. Meanwhile, her travels meant delaying graduation by an academic quarter and leaving behind her boyfriend of one year, Jeremy Kane, a star Stanford swimmer (and White House summer intern). Friends weren't concerned about the separation. "They're in it for the long haul," said classmate Anthony Robinson. While Mom rode the campaign trail, Chelsea, 20, also lent a hand in the final months of her father's presidency. In March they made an official visit to India. In July she served as a hostess at a state dinner for Morocco's King Mohammed VI. At both, she earned raves. Said former White House social secretary Letitia Baldrige: "She does America proud."

On a New Zealand holiday, Zara Phillips, 18, the daughter of Britain's Princess Anne, bungee-jumped off a bridge near Queensland. There's no indication that Zara (left, before the leap) was able to cajole other royals into joining her for an exhilarating plunge.

PARTY ANIMALS

OSCARS

Billy Crystal, back at his hosting post, provided one of the few familiar faces onstage as first-timers like Hilary Swank and *Girl, Interrupted*'s Angelina Jolie claimed the gold. But with gobs of glamor, even the ingenues proved they could dress the part

In the indie flick *Boys Don't Cry*, Hilary Swank plays a young woman who wants to be a guy and pays with her life for the choice. But when she stepped up to the podium to accept her Best Actress award, in tinkly diamonds and a bronze gown by Randolph Duke, she made it clear that she's all girl.

Meanwhile, out on the red carpet, Trey "Jennifer" Parker and Matt "Gwyneth" Stone, creators of *South Park: Bigger, Longer, Uncut* (with the film's also-nominated composer, Marc Shaiman), bent gender in some familiar frocks.

No nominations yet for newcomer Kate Hudson, who shines in *Almost Famous* and *Dr. T and the Women.* But she adorned a post-awards party, showing off a bippy that could become as famous as her mom's.

Brad Pitt and still bride-to-be Jennifer Aniston took in the scene, which included his ex, Gwyneth Paltrow. She hung out with Matt Damon and his girlfriend, Winona Ryder.

Singer-actress Erykah Badu, who appeared in the nominated *Cider House Rules,* wore two different green dresses during the night, a matching head wrap and a ropy necklace she designed herself. "It makes me feel very comfortable," she assured onlookers.

Friends and competitors for Best Actress, Meryl Streep and Julianne Moore made kissy face after both left empty-handed.

Holding his metallic-draped wife, Pauletta, was the closest Best Actor nominee Denzel Washington came to a gold figure that night. His work in *The Hurricane* got lost in the *American Beauty* sweep.

The Oscars

72ND ANNUAL ACADEMY AWARDS

(Presented March 26, 2000)
Picture: *American Beauty* Actor: Kevin Spacey, *American Beauty* Actress: Hilary Swank, *Boys Don't Cry* Supporting Actor: Michael Caine, *The Cider House Rules* Supporting Actress: Angelina Jolie, *Girl, Interrupted* Director: Sam Mendes, *American Beauty* Original Screenplay: Alan Ball, *American Beauty* Adapted Screenplay: John Irving, *The Cider House Rules* Original Song: Phil Collins, "You'll Be in My Heart," *Tarzan* Cinematography: Conrad Hall, *American Beauty* Original Dramatic Score: John Corigliano, *The Red Violin* Documentary: Arthur Cohn, *One Day in September* Honorary Award: Andrzej Wajda Irving Thalberg Memorial Award: Warren Beatty

Lance Bass of 'N Sync sported the monochromatic look popularized by Regis Philbin. Bass performed "The Music of My Heart" with Gloria Estefan, up for Best Song. "We're all movie buffs," he said of his boy-band pals.

At the DreamWorks bash, *American Beauty*'s Thora Birch (center) and Mena Suvari celebrated with costar Kevin Spacey. "I'm still stunned," he said of winning his second Oscar in four years.

GOLDEN GLOBES

"Donatella Versace came through for me," said Hilary Swank, at the first of several awards shows that she would dominate.

The splendor of a simple Calvin Klein dress and her beau, Benjamin Bratt, made Julia Roberts a pretty happy woman.

Felicity's Keri Russell solved the high-heel problem by kicking hers off to dance at the DreamWorks after-party at Trader Vic's.

Partying with *Sopranos* costar Edie Falco, James Gandolfini said he looked forward to "a long nap" following the awards.

Do couples in love start to look alike? Or, as with Winona Ryder and Matt Damon, is it just their haircuts that seem identical?

68

Though Kevin Spacey caught her eye, Courtney Love turned heads with her shredded silk taffeta by John Galliano. "Aren't I subversive?" joked the rocker-actress.

Her *Sex and the City* coup rendered Sarah Jessica Parker speechless. Coming to, she said, "I don't ever recall winning [even] a spelling bee!"

The Golden Globes

57TH ANNUAL GOLDEN GLOBE AWARDS
(Presented January 23, 2000)

MOTION PICTURES
Drama: *American Beauty* Actor, Drama: Denzel Washington, *The Hurricane* Actress, Drama: Hilary Swank, *Boys Don't Cry* Musical or Comedy: *Toy Story 2* Actor, Musical or Comedy: Jim Carrey, *Man on the Moon* Actress, Musical or Comedy: Janet McTeer, *Tumbleweeds* Supporting Actor: Tom Cruise, *Magnolia* Supporting Actress: Angelina Jolie, *Girl, Interrupted* Director: Sam Mendes, *American Beauty* Screenplay: *American Beauty*

TELEVISION
Drama Series: *The Sopranos* Actor, Drama Series: James Gandolfini, *The Sopranos* Actress, Drama Series: Edie Falco, *The Sopranos* Musical Comedy or Series: *Sex and the City* Actor, Musical or Comedy Series: Michael J. Fox, *Spin City* Actress, Musical Comedy or Series: Sarah Jessica Parker, *Sex and the City*

EMMYS

The flashy fabric didn't sell Patricia Heaton on her ornate Dolce & Gabbana gown. "It had to be comfortable," she said.

Her attendance here proved that film refugee Geena Davis was ready for prime time, even if her see-through test-pattern dress was not quite.

Sex and the City's Sarah Jessica Parker exulted of her pink, ostrich-feather Oscar de la Renta confection, "It's my fantasy dress."

Exiting *Spin City* star Michael J. Fox escorted wife Tracy Pollan. "Whenever I see pictures of us," he said, "I always think, 'Who is that lucky little short guy?'"

A first-time winner for her role on *Once and Again*, Sela Ward called her David Cardona leather outfit "a fun change of pace."

The Emmys

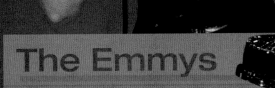

52ND ANNUAL EMMY AWARDS
(Presented September 10, 2000)
Drama Series: *The West Wing* Comedy Series: *Will & Grace* Variety, Music or Comedy Series: *Late Show with David Letterman* Miniseries: *The Corner* Actor, Drama: James Gandolfini, *The Sopranos* Actress, Drama: Sela Ward, *Once and Again* Actor, Comedy: Michael J. Fox, *Spin City* Actress, Comedy: Patricia Heaton, *Everybody Loves Raymond* Actor, Miniseries or Special: Jack Lemmon, *Tuesdays with Morrie* Actress, Miniseries or Special: Halle Berry, *Introducing Dorothy Dandridge* Supporting Actor, Drama: Richard Schiff, *The West Wing* Supporting Actress, Drama: Allison Janney, *The West Wing* Supporting Actor, Comedy: Sean Hayes, *Will & Grace* Supporting Actress, Comedy: Megan Mullally, *Will & Grace* Supporting Actor, Miniseries or Special: Hank Azaria, *Tuesdays with Morrie* Supporting Actress, Miniseries or Special: Vanessa Redgrave, *If These Walls Could Talk 2*

"I feel like a movie star," said small-screen star Allison Janney, lapping up the attention of her *West Wing* commander-in-chief, Martin Sheen.

71

GRAMMYS

Grammys

42ND ANNUAL GRAMMY AWARDS

(Presented February 23, 2000)

Record of the Year: *Supernatural*, Santana
Song of the Year: "Smooth," Santana
Album of the Year: *Supernatural*, Santana
New Artist: Christina Aguilera Male Pop Vocal: "Brand New Day," Sting Female Pop Vocal: "I Will Remember You," Sarah McLachlan Pop Vocal by a Duo or Group: "Smooth," Santana, featuring Rob Thomas Pop Album: *Brand New Day*, Sting Rock Song: "Scar Tissue," Red Hot Chili Peppers Male Rock Vocal: "American Woman," Lenny Kravitz Female Rock Vocal: "Sweet Child o' Mine," Sheryl Crow Rock Vocal by a Duo or Group: "Put Your Lights On," Santana, featuring Everlast R&B Song: "No Scrubs," TLC Rap Solo: "My Name Is," Eminem

Is Whitney Houston happy about her win, or because Emanuel Ungaro found the only pink fox in the forest?

Versace dress? Check. Jeweled brooch? Check. Double-sided tape? Check, check. If you were Jennifer Lopez this year, you wondered how you ever got dressed without it.

"I'm just trying to be loud, that's all," explained Macy Gray of her vivid Perry White coat.

Everybody loves a dad who takes you to meet pop stars, as Ray Romano's kid Alexandra knows.

LATIN GRAMMYS

Mexican-born Carlos Santana (with presenter Andy Garcia) cleaned up at both Grammys this year. Each win, he said, "feels like the first kiss."

The envelope, *por favor.* Jennifer Lopez, who co-hosted with Jimmy Smits, was to perform her duet with Marc Anthony, a last-minute no-show.

"This is a way for me to explore my Latin roots," said nominee Christina Aguilera, whose dad comes from Ecuador.

Multinational couple Antonio Banderas and Melanie Griffith bravoed a show that paid tribute to one of Latin music's legends, Tito Puente.

FIRST ANNUAL LATIN GRAMMY AWARDS
(Presented September 13, 2000)

Record: *Corazón Espinado,* Santana, featuring Maná Album: *Amarte Es un Placer,* Luis Miguel Song: "Dímelo," Marc Anthony, Robert Blades, Angie Chirino, Cory Rooney Best New Artist: Ibrahim Ferrer Female Pop Vocal: "Ojos Así," Shakira Male Pop Vocal: "Tu Mirada," Luis Miguel Pop Duo or Group: "Se Me Olvidó Otra Vez," Maná Pop Instrumental: "El Farol," Santana Female Rock Vocal: "Octavo Dia," Shakira Male Rock Vocal: "Al Lado del Camino," Fito Páez Rock Duo or Group: "Corazón Espinado," Santana, featuring Maná

CMA

The CMAs

THE 34TH ANNUAL COUNTRY MUSIC AWARDS

(Presented October 4, 2000)
Entertainer: Dixie Chicks Male Vocalist: Tim McGraw Female Vocalist: Faith Hill Single: "I Hope You Dance," Lee Ann Womack Album: *Fly*, Dixie Chicks Vocal Group: Dixie Chicks Vocal Duo: Montgomery Gentry Music Video: "Goodbye Earl," Dixie Chicks Horizon Award: Brad Paisley Event: George Strait with Alan Jackson, *Murder on Music Row*

Nominee Tim McGraw said of his wife, singer Faith Hill, "I would rather have not won if Faith hadn't won."

Perpetual partygoer Lance Bass of 'N Sync appeared out of his musical bag with country teen star LeAnn Rimes.

Shania Twain's "highlight" was seeing the Dixie Chicks. (The hope of singer Billy Gilman, 12, was to see Twain.)

Emily Robison (left) and Martie Seidel laid hands on fellow Dixie Chick and mom-to-be Natalie Maines. All wore vintage Giorgio di Sant'Angelo.

Yes, it's real. Tom Hanks, sporting the latest in deserted-island facial hair fashions, attended on a break from the shooting of his new film, *Cast Away*.

Dressed in Versace, Angelina Jolie took the surprisingly sensible step of asking a friend to "make sure my tattoos didn't show."

SAG
The SAG Awards

6TH ANNUAL SCREEN ACTORS GUILD AWARDS

(Presented March 12, 2000)
FILM Actor: Kevin Spacey, *American Beauty* Actress: Annette Bening, *American Beauty* Supporting Actor: Michael Caine, *The Cider House Rules* Supporting Actress: Angelina Jolie, *Girl, Interrupted* Motion Picture Cast: *American Beauty*
TELEVISION Actor, Movie or Miniseries: Jack Lemmon, *Oprah Winfrey Presents: Tuesdays with Morrie* Actress, Movie or Miniseries: Halle Berry, *Introducing Dorothy Dandridge* Actor, Drama Series: James Gandolfini, *The Sopranos* Actress, Drama Series: Edie Falco, *The Sopranos* Actor, Comedy Series: Michael J. Fox, *Spin City* Actress, Comedy Series: Lisa Kudrow, *Friends* Ensemble, Drama Series: *The Sopranos* Ensemble, Comedy Series: *Frasier* Lifetime Achievement Award: Sidney Poitier

Hilary Swank looked just that in a Randolph Duke gown. Despite the sparkly smile, she admitted, "I can't breathe."

With *Friends* pal Jennifer Aniston, Lisa Kudrow explained the dynamics of her dress this way: "It just stays up somehow."

MTV

The MTV Video Music Awards

After enduring months of rumors that she had a drug problem, a serene, smiling and be-furred Whitney Houston attended as a presenter with husband Bobby Brown.

The punctuationally challenged 'N Sync took the stage to deliver their ubiquitous hit "Bye Bye Bye," but went home at the end of the night empty-handed.

17TH ANNUAL MTV VIDEO MUSIC AWARDS
(Presented September 7, 2000)
Video: Eminem, "The Real Slim Shady" Male Video: Eminem, "The Real Slim Shady Female Video: Aaliyah, "Try Again" Group Video: Blink-182, "All The Small Things" R&B Video: Destiny's Child, "Say My Name" Rap Video: Dr. Dre, featuring Eminem, "Forget About Dre" Hip-Hop Video: Sisqó, "Thong Song" Dance Video: Jennifer Lopez, "Waiting for Tonight" Rock Video: Limp Bizkit, "Break Stuff" New Artist: Macy Gray, "I Try"

Britney Spears first appeared in a black suit to sing "(I Can't Get No) Satisfaction," a song older than she is. She then ripped off that outfit to reveal this one for her hit "Oops . . . I Did It Again."

Wondering aloud why he was there since he is neither a music nor video artist, Jim Carrey plugged his upcoming *Grinch* film and, well, waved his butt around for all to enjoy.

Eminem entered the auditorium with a sea of bleached-blond look-alikes to perform that catchy ode to his alter ego, "The Real Slim Shady."

No one from sudden star Macy Gray to tennis sensations Venus and Serena Williams was safe from cohosts Shawn and Marlon Wayans' wicked barbs.

The MTV Movie Awards

NINTH ANNUAL MTV MOVIE AWARDS

(Presented June 3, 2000)
Film: *The Matrix* Actor: Keanu Reeves, *The Matrix* Actress: Sarah Michelle Gellar, *Cruel Intentions* Best Comedic Performance: Adam Sandler, *Big Daddy* Best Breakthrough Performances: Haley Joel Osment, *The Sixth Sense*, and Julia Stiles, *10 Things I Hate About You* Best Villain: Mike Myers, *Austin Powers: The Spy Who Shagged Me* Best Kiss: Sarah Michelle Gellar and Selma Blair, *Cruel Intentions* Best Fight: Keanu Reeves vs. Laurence Fishburne, *The Matrix*

Beadazzler Halle Berry presented one of MTV's "golden popcorn" statues.

Freddie Prinze Jr. cuddled Sarah Michelle Gellar, a cowinner of Best Kiss.

Matrix stars Carrie-Anne Moss and Keanu Reeves hung with Mel Gibson.

As *Sex and the City*'s four Manhattan power chicks incessantly debate whether size really matters (in shocking MA-TV detail), the stars of cable's breakout hit have found that, yes, bigger and broader is better

SENSATIONS

"Most shows are lucky to have one strong woman [character]," said Kristin Davis of the *Sex and the City* cast (from left, Kim Cattrall, Davis, Sarah Jessica Parker and Cynthia Nixon). "We have four, and I'm very proud of that."

With her three gal pals, Sarah Jessica Parker talks a blue streak to success

"What if Prince Charming had never shown up? Would Snow White have slept in that glass coffin forever? Or would she have eventually woken up, spit out the apple, gotten a job, a health-care package and a baby from her local neighborhood sperm bank?" Fictional sex columnist Carrie Bradshaw posed that fairy-tale proposition, and some 10.6 million viewers tune in weekly for the answer. In the third season of HBO's *Sex and the City,* Bradshaw (Sarah Jessica Parker) and her three boy-obsessed girlfriends somehow proved that Mr. Right is less essential than the right shoes, preferably spiky Manolo Blahniks. Based on the musings of real-life columnist Candace Bushnell, the racy show broke ground by, at last, depicting unmarrieds as something more than desperate seekers.

But though 54 percent of its devotees claim that *Sex* is a realistic representation of single life, its stars hardly relate at all. Parker, 35, is happily married to actor Matthew Broderick. When she's working 16-hour days, she suspects that her husband of three years "doesn't have his laundry done [and] hasn't had a hot meal in days. That stuff weighs on my mind." So, too, does her desire to have a child. Kim Cattrall, who plays the undisputed biggest bed-hopper on the show, is also married. "At this point," says Cattrall, 44, "I expected to be playing moms and wives. It's exciting to play a femme fatale." Costar Cynthia Nixon, 34, lives with the father of her 4-year-old daughter Samantha but, like her relationship-phobic character, has no plans to wed. Kristin Davis, 35, who portrays the most marriage-minded of the four, is in reality the only dedicated dater. But she's like the prude she portrays in that the scripts often make her flinch. She admits to blushing and warning her mother not to watch certain episodes. Homebody Parker, however, is proud of her sexy alter ego. "I'm a New Yorker," she said. "And it's always great to see yourself in a billboard."

Yankee fan Parker took in the World Series with hubby Matthew Broderick (above), but on her show, will she take the plunge with "Mr. Big" (Chris Noth, right)?

MALCOLM'S MUNIZ IS ON TOP

New Jersey kid Frankie Muniz says, "It's been my dream to have my own television show since I was little." This year he got his wish, and more. Besides the title role in FOX's *Malcolm in the Middle,* he could be seen on the big screen in *My Dog Skip.* When he learned he'd landed *Malcolm,* "I got on the bed and started yelling and jumping," recalls Muniz, 14. But his mom, Denise, who has homeschooled Frankie since sixth grade, has kept him "grounded." That means the young headliner still has to make his bed.

They Cried Her a River

After teary concerts on both coasts—'Like buttah!' raved fans—Barbra Streisand called it quits. And this time, she said, she means it

Goldie's Girl

A Hollywood scion came into her own as *Almost Famous* made Kate Hudson just that

After her giggly days on TV's *Laugh-In,* Goldie Hawn might have had a tough road carving out a film career. But on her first try she won an Oscar. Now the only hurdle her daughter Kate Hudson faces is distinguishing herself from her famous family. (Her father is '70s TV host Bill Hudson, but actor Kurt Russell is the man she calls Dad.) Hudson, 21, dealt with the issue by never denying it. With a knowing wink, she donned body graffiti for a *Laugh-In* send-up on *Saturday Night Live.* But her turn as a groupie in *Almost Famous* proved she has her own talent in abundance. Now Hawn can focus on other motherly concerns. Dating Black Crowes singer Chris Robinson, Hudson reports, "My whole family is like, 'Kate, don't mess this one up.'"

To say Linda Richman was *verklempt* really doesn't begin to approach it. Mike Myers' über-Streisand fan surely became momentarily hysterical on hearing her idol was leaving the stage forever. Married for two years to actor James Brolin, Streisand, 58, said she would continue making albums and movies but was retiring her live act in order to have "more time to live life." The announcement sent ticket prices for the L.A. and New York shows soaring to $2,500 for the best seats. But plenty of the diva's devotees were willing to pay. John Travolta. Lauren Bacall. Rosie O'Donnell. Regis Philbin. Jesse Jackson. Madeleine Albright. Barbara Walters. Sidney Poitier. Sarah Jessica Parker. And Salma Hayek (who flew her mother in from Mexico, because "it was her dream to see her all her life").

By all accounts, the girl from Brooklyn did not disappoint, taking concertgoers on a musical journey from her first recording as a kid and on through her Broadway and movie hits. The only criticism was leveled at the schmaltzy photo album projected overhead. But most fans were too rapt to complain. As they took in the closing bars of "People," her last song, they could sit satisfied in the knowledge that they may have witnessed a legend's final bow. Will Streisand ever take the stage again? As Linda Richman would say, "Talk amongst yourselves."

Philbin (backstage with Gifford on her last day) says he'll miss her "spunk and spontaneity." Her spot on the couch had barely cooled when Sarah Ferguson filled it in September (right). Would she consider the job permanently? "Absolutely," said the Duchess. "If they offer it."

Broadcast Bachelor

Who will replace Kathie Lee? Regis Philbin readies his final answer

All good things must come to an end. So, too, must endearingly/maddeningly perky things. Thus on Leap Year Day, Kathie Lee Gifford, she of the caffeinated early-morning smile, announced she was breaking up the team that hosted *Live! with Regis and Kathie Lee* for 15 years. Her decision, said Gifford, 47, came from a desire "to make different dreams come true." Those dreams include acting (she shot a TV movie with her son and favorite talk topic, Cody) and singing (she cut a new album, *Heart of a Woman*).

While Philbin, 68, disputed rumors that he beseeched her to stay, the more curmudgeonly half of *Live!* did get teary during Gifford's last show in August. But like Prince Charming toting a glass slipper around his morning-talk kingdom, Philbin proceeded to share his couch with a parade of hopefuls that included Dolly Parton, assorted *Survivor* cast members, his wife Joy and the Duchess of York. "We're not really going to be able to replace Kathie Lee," said producer Michael Gelman. But curiously, ratings rose 26 percent after she left.

OPRAH INTRODUCES HER ARTICLES OF FAITH

Always mindful of the spiritual and intellectual welfare of her millions of devotees, Oprah Winfrey provided them with something to read between book-club selections. Like *Martha Stewart Living* before it, *O: The Oprah Magazine* put its celebrity editor on the cover and filled its pages with tips for making the reader's élan more like her own, such as "Live your best life! Start right here, right now!" Winfrey's own best life included a magazine launch party (below) with exemplars Rosie O'Donnell and Tina Turner.

Under Her Spell

Thirty-five mil have read J.K. Rowling's Harry Potter. Only one will get to be him

English author J.K. Rowling, 34, swears she had no idea how big a phenomenon Harry Potter would become. By the time the first three books had been translated into a 35th language, the divorced former welfare mom began to have some notion, and wanted the fourth installment—the darker *Goblet of Fire*—to premiere in an appropriately splashy way. So she asked her publisher to embargo the 735-pager from reviewers until midnight on its July 8 release date and let kids get it first. And they did, preordering 282,000 copies on Amazon.com alone, and crowding with their parents into bookstores that stayed open until the witching hours. Meanwhile, Rowling's domination of the *New York Times* bestseller list forced a spin-off of kiddie lit so that adult fiction could again top the chart. "Like life, but better" is how one young reader explained the allure of the boy wizard from Hogwarts School. Many adults agreed. Others shook their heads but were nonetheless pleased to see their kids reading rather than playing video games or sitting in a tube-induced stupor. A few muggles (that's humans in Potterspeak) got the series banned from schools due to its occult content. But Harrymania marches on. A film adaptation is due in November 2001.

During a lengthy search for a flesh-and-blood Harry, Rowling (right, on the book tour) joked that she was tempted to "lunge at [some] kid and say 'Can you act? You're coming with me. Taxi!'" Finally, Daniel Radcliffe (above, in Potter specs) won the part; Emma Watson and Rupert Grint will play his pals.

Teen Dream

Too many pop princesses? Not! Moore's the merrier, says Mandy

Oops, they did it again. The pop packagers in Orlando—the same ones who built the careers of Britney Spears and 'N Sync—launched another big act, this one only 16. But music and video star Mandy Moore says she's different from Spears or Christina Aguilera, since she won't push her records by wearing skimpy outfits. "I'm not comfortable doing that," says Moore, who followed her platinum-seller *So Real* with this year's *I Wanna Be with You*. She *is* comfortable singing flirty love songs, though she doesn't have a boyfriend yet. "I'd love to have somebody in mind when I sing," she sighed. Still, her booming career must cheer her, right? "When people say 'You made it,' I think, 'But I'm not done yet. Not everyone's heard my music.' I want to be a household name."

Lemme See It!

A song in the key of G-string makes Sisqó a new R&B star

There are love songs more romantic—and eloquent. But for sincerity, it's hard to doubt his depth of feeling when Sisqó sings, "Baby make your booty go/ Baby I know you wanna show/ That thong thong thong thong thong." Women fall into two camps regarding thongs. You love 'em (no panty lines!) or hate 'em (wedgies!). Sisqó's sentiments are unequivocal. According to his megahit "The Thong Song," he adores them. And he wants to see them. As a result, female fans have been making like Monica Lewinsky and flashing their thongs at Sisqó (born Mark Andrews, 22 years ago), even when he's out with his 5-year-old. "This girl wanted to show me her thong," recalled Sisqó. "I covered my daughter's eyes." Still, while he's enjoying his success, it has cost him. During the song's racy video shoot, his girlfriend left him, thong and all.

More Than Just Pretty Women

Erin Brockovich's legal win provides Julia Roberts another box-office score

Mostly, they got it right, says Erin Brockovich, subject of the eponymous film. It's accurate that she, as a financially struggling, twice-divorced mother of three, groveled for a job at a Los Angeles law firm which she eventually helped win one of the biggest class-action suits in history. And it's true that she often talks more like a longshoreman and dresses more like a cocktail waitress than a legal clerk. But never, she insists, does she let her bra strap peek out from her blouse as Julia Roberts did onscreen. Eight years ago, Brockovich dug up the research that helped collect a $333 million judgment against Pacific Gas & Electric, charged with polluting a town's water supply with chromium and causing a spate of illnesses from nosebleeds to cancer.

"She's more than a great body," said Valerie Bruce, a complainant in the suit. "She's smart, honest and forthcoming." The combination of her scrappy determination, big heart, and knockout looks made her a natural for film—and for Roberts, 32, who was still buoyant from successes in *Runaway Bride* and *Notting Hill,* as well as her deepening relationship with actor Benjamin Bratt, 36. "I was catching her at a real high point," said *Brockovich* director Steven Soderbergh. The film earned more than $125 million, burnished Roberts's star with a Norma Rae–meets–Barbie performance, and made Brockovich, 39, a celebrity herself. That development brought trouble, however, when one of her exes and a former boyfriend tried unsuccessfully to extort $300,000 from Brockovich, now remarried and back at the law firm. Though she clearly loved being part of Roberts's world—attending the premiere and appearing together on *Oprah*—her acting career ended with a walk-on in the film as a waitress named Julia.

Called by a pal "maternal and loving," Roberts captured single mom Brockovich (left) but in life is still just dating Benjamin Bratt.

Working with sick plaintiffs "taught me the value of family," remarks Brockovich (at home in L.A.). Indeed, she says of her new husband, actor Eric Ellis, 34, "he was able to stop the chaos [in my life]."

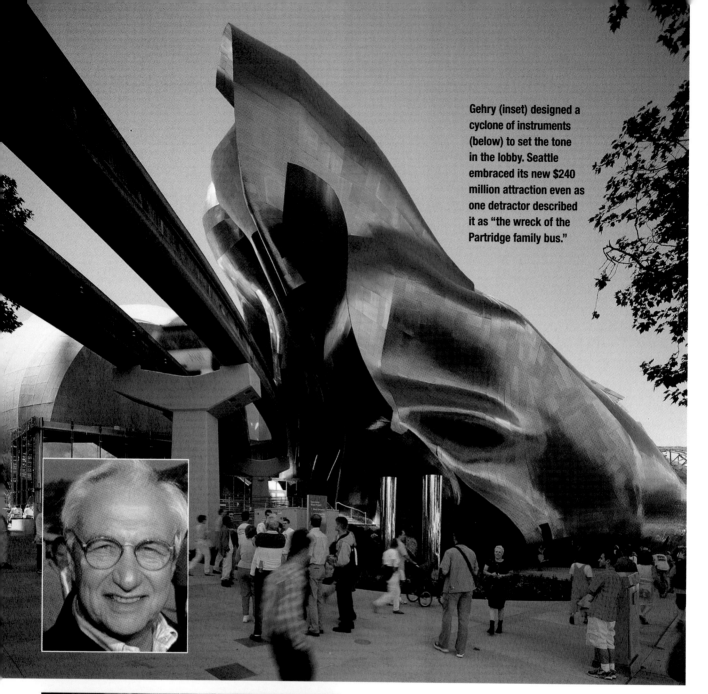

Gehry (inset) designed a cyclone of instruments (below) to set the tone in the lobby. Seattle embraced its new $240 million attraction even as one detractor described it as "the wreck of the Partridge family bus."

Ode to Jimi

Frank Gehry builds on Paul Allen's obsession to create a museum that rocks

Microsoft cofounder Paul Allen loves Seattle native Jimi Hendrix and rock so much that he commissioned a museum—the Experience Music Project—to pay homage at the foot of the town's Space Needle. Inside, visitors would not only see Allen's personal collection but also, in interactive galleries, get the feel of performing before a crowd. The billionaire, who has his own rock band, enlisted Frank Gehry, the architect behind the instantly iconic Guggenheim Museum in Bilbao, Spain. A 71-year-old jazz fan, Gehry got into the groove, smashing guitars like Pete Townshend and producing a design that throbs like a three-chord anthem. "Before that," he admits, "I didn't know what a wa-wa pedal was." The museum will now solve this mystery for the world.

KING OF CLUBS

This year, golf's best player only got better. He took the U.S. Open by a record-breaking 15 strokes, ran away with the British Open and won the PGA in a heart-stopping play-off. That made Tiger the first player since Ben Hogan in 1953 to collect three grand-slam titles in a year. When he wasn't astounding the golf world or signing heaps of autographs, he made time for other passions, including video games and, most of all, steady girl-friend Joanna Jagoda, 22, a California poli sci major (right, with Woods's mother, Tida). He also hosted fund-raisers and golf clinics for his kids' charity, the Tiger Woods Foundation. And he pondered the dream manse he plans to build on his golf earnings ($17 million so far), not touching his $100 mil endorsement swag. Though he has reinforced his own legend at 24, his head has not been turned. In June the pro of pros showed up at an amateur tourney—as a caddy for his former Stanford roommate.

OKAY, NOBODY MOVE!

When Madame Tussaud throws a party, all the A-listers show up. . . . Though it's not as if they have much choice. Their attendance is ensured by the sculpting team at this, the first American branch of the Madame's London Wax Museum. With the flagship location still drawing 2.7 million visitors each year, Tussaud's opened a $50 million outpost in New York's Times Square. The five-story museum features 175 full-time celebrities-in-residence, including, from left, *Today* show hosts Al Roker and Matt Lauer, Cybill Shepherd, Hugh Grant, Woody Allen, John Travolta, Oprah Winfrey, RuPaul (on the half shell), Brad Pitt, Tony Bennett, Jodie Foster, Yoko Ono and Elton John. (Prior to the opening, artist Rachel Wade, right, put the finishing touches on the sexiest man, um, sort-of-alive.) To cooperate in their cloning, the living legends submit to numerous measurements and photographs. At a preview, Tony Bennett was understandably alarmed by his likeness "looking right at me." Melanie "Scary Spice" Brown professed to be "very impressed with her backside," says a staffer. Indeed. Without her ever making another trip to the gym, her wax derriere will forever resist gravity and aging. Just don't get too close to the fire, Scary.

Becoming Friends for Life

On their wedding day, Brad and Jennifer light up the sky with a display worthy of a Hollywood premiere

"Spectacular," pronounced objective observer papa John Aniston (opposite, top, with Jennifer and her half brother John Melick). Bill and Jane Pitt (center) flew in from Missouri to see their son and his bride exchange white gold wedding bands (above). The couple "wanted a memorable event," said Lt. Thom Bradstock of the presiding sheriff's department, and the drama unfolded under tents to foil the paparazzi.

THEY MEET, THEY MATE, AND SOMETIMES THEY PART

FAMILY MATTERS

Wedding with four bands, a gospel choir, 50,000 flowers, dinner for 200 and fireworks: $1,000,000.

Penalty levied against hired hands who violated their confidentiality agreements and leaked details of said nuptials: $100,000.

Joining in holy fabulosity of Mr. and Mrs. Sexiest Man Alive: Priceless.

On a Malibu bluff, Brad Pitt, 36, whose romantic CV includes liaisons with Gwyneth Paltrow and Juliette Lewis, pledged to spend forever with Jennifer Aniston, 31, the *Friends* star whose hair launched a thousand shags. Before family and friends (including all of her TV costars except Matt LeBlanc, who was on movie location in Budapest), Aniston promised to always make Pitt his favorite banana milk shakes, while he vowed to split the difference with her on the contentious thermostat issue. (Aniston's mother, estranged from her daughter ever since giving a negative interview to a tabloid show, was not invited.)

Escorted down the aisle by her father, soap actor John Aniston, the bride looked luminous in a glass-beaded silk gown by Milan designer Lawrence Steele, while Pitt donned a tuxedo from Parisian Hedi Slimane. After their first kiss as husband and wife, dancing broke out to music by a Greek bouzouki band, a Latin jazz combo, a 12-year-old Sinatra-style singer and, at one point, actor Dermot Mulroney on the mandolin and Melissa Etheridge covering Led Zeppelin. Then came a fireworks show over the Pacific. "There were big expectations," said Aniston's hairstylist, Chris McMillan. "And this went way beyond that. Way beyond."

95

'Harry and I Are Both Quite Upset'

Prince William speaks for the first time about the press's treatment of his mother

Three years after her death, there seems to be no lessening of interest in Princess Diana. In March her former bodyguard Trevor Rees-Jones, the only survivor of the crash that took her life and that of boyfriend Dodi Fayed, put out a book detailing the princess's final days. He said he hoped his account would provide "a sense of closure" for her sons, Princes William, 18, and Harry, 16. "I wouldn't want to put

them through any more grief."

Later in the year a former aide to Diana published another book with no such demonstrable regard. Patrick Jephson's *Shadows of a Princess* depicted his boss as childish, manipulative, paranoid and vindictive. This portrayal cut close enough to the core to make William, who had never addressed the press on the topic before, speak out about his mother. Standing outside his father's Highgrove estate

on an autumn day (below), he fielded questions from a group of 15 or so preselected journalists and offered answers that had been vetted by Buckingham Palace. Without citing Jephson's book by name, one reporter asked William about "recent press coverage."

"Of course, Harry and I are both quite upset," he said directly, "that our mother's trust has been betrayed and that even now she is still being exploited. I don't really want to say

any more than that." Making the statement, said a Palace source, "was a difficult decision" for the prince. But he was more at ease discussing his own relationship with the press while at Eton. "They have been very good," he said. "I hope it just continues for Harry."

Before leaving Eton, William posed for pictures to mark his 18th birthday, June 21. In one, he prepared paella for a cooking course, and confided that he was one of "the world's worst cooks." Still, his mum might be proud of his conduct, if not of his culinary skills.

HAPPY 100TH BIRTHDAY, MA'AM

Long before Diana, the most popular British royal was the wife of King George VI. She spun even the bombing of Buckingham Palace into a positive, saying, "It makes me feel I can look the East End in the face." So as she turned 100, the Queen Mother was again the world's favorite Windsor. She still pays official visits and throws great parties. "She's the best advertisement for gin in the world," jokes a friend. Said another of the Queen Mum, who kicked up her heels until 2 a.m. at one of several centenary bashes: "Her secret is her joy in life."

Going to the Chapel

Longtime loves and at least one stealth pair (yo, Boltin' Billy Bob!) take the plunge

While still supposedly with Laura Dern ("It's like a sudden death," Dern later told *Talk*), Billy Bob Thornton, 44, eloped with Angelina Jolie, 24, at the not-so-lucky Vegas chapel where Cindy Crawford had wed Richard Gere.

After a reception attended by 100 people, Noah Wyle, 28, and his bride, makeup artist Tracy Warbin, 32, hosted an intimate gathering for a few friends at their California ranch that lasted into the next day.

TV producer Ryan Haddon, 29, toted a traditional bouquet down the aisle, while groom Christian Slater, 30, carried the couple's 10-month-old son Jaden. At the altar, they exchanged roses along with their rings.

"Figure skaters have awful perceptions of hockey players. I thought, 'This guy's a little different,'" said Olympic gold medalist Kristi Yamaguchi, 29, of meeting Bret Hedican, also 29, of the Florida Panthers. After five years of dating, they sealed the deal in Hawaii.

THE BACKSTREET BRIDES

Preteen hearts skipped a couple of beats this year when two-fifths of the Backstreet Boys got hitched. Kevin Richardson, 28, married Kristin Willits, 29 (top), a dancer he met while working as a costumed character at a theme park in 1993. "It's great he became what he is," said the bride's mother, Susan Patton. "But we knew him when he was a Ninja Turtle." Three months later, Richardson's bandmate and cousin Brian Littrell, 25, wed his girlfriend of three years, actress Leighanne Wallace, 31. Outside the Atlanta church, throngs of fans waited for a glimpse of arriving guests, including the three still-single Backstreeters.

The bride bore flowers and the groom wore "a smile as wide as Texas," said one guest at the al-fresco wedding of country stars Amy Grant, 39, and Vince Gill, 42.

Muhammed Ali is now a father and father-in-law to a boxer. His daughter Laila, 22, a pioneer for women in the sport, married champ Johnny McClain, 32.

Sweethearts since New York University grad school, Debra Messing, 32, and screenwriter Daniel Zelman, 33, made it offi-cial in a beachside ceremony attended by 150, among them her pals from *Will & Grace*.

"Lightning doesn't usually strike twice," said real estate mogul Marshall Rose, 63, at his marriage to Candice Bergen, 54. Both lost their first spouse to cancer.

Fish everywhere rethought the utility of bicycles when feminist Gloria Steinem, 66, wed entrepreneur David Bale, 61, dad to *American Psycho* star Christian.

Wed in a small ceremony, Emeril Lagasse, 40, and real estate broker Alden Lovelace, 33, kicked the fête up a notch the next day, with 500 people at one of the chef's New Orleans eateries.

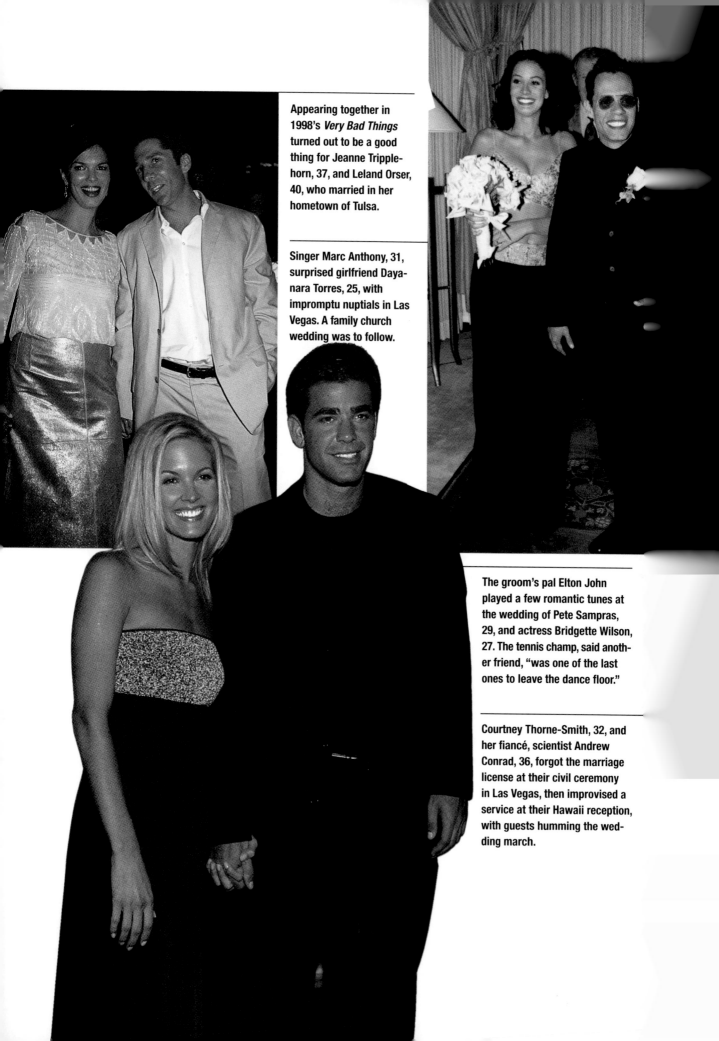

Appearing together in 1998's *Very Bad Things* turned out to be a good thing for Jeanne Tripplehorn, 37, and Leland Orser, 40, who married in her hometown of Tulsa.

Singer Marc Anthony, 31, surprised girlfriend Dayanara Torres, 25, with impromptu nuptials in Las Vegas. A family church wedding was to follow.

The groom's pal Elton John played a few romantic tunes at the wedding of Pete Sampras, 29, and actress Bridgette Wilson, 27. The tennis champ, said another friend, "was one of the last ones to leave the dance floor."

Courtney Thorne-Smith, 32, and her fiancé, scientist Andrew Conrad, 36, forgot the marriage license at their civil ceremony in Las Vegas, then improvised a service at their Hawaii reception, with guests humming the wedding march.

At the wedding of Revlon chief Ron Perelman, 57, and actress Ellen Barkin, 46, the guests included his six kids from three prior marriages, her two children and ex-husband Gabriel Byrne, who "wished them every joy."

American Beauty star Mena Suvari, 21 (below, at the Academy Awards), secretly wed cinematographer Robert (*The Cable Guy*) Brinkman, 38, in March but didn't spill the beans for a month.

You've Got Heirs!

The world welcomes a lot of little people who have no idea their folks are famous

"It's fabulous! It's sensational! It's another beauty for the world!" raved fashion photographer Francesco Scavullo, a friend of new parents Iman, 45, and David Bowie, 53. On August 15 the model-turned-cosmetics-mogul and the gentrified glam rocker welcomed Alexandria.

Nine months earlier, Kelly Preston, 37, shared the impending good news with husband John Travolta, 46, by wrapping her positive pregnancy-test stick as a present. "I guess it wasn't romantic, but it was funny," she said. On April 3 Ella Bleu joined a family that also includes brother Jett, 8.

After the February 6 delivery of son Homer, dad Richard Gere, 50, who played a sensitive obstetrician in *Dr. T & the Women,* boasted, "I could have done it myself." Perhaps. But mom Carey Lowell, 39 (right, with Gere and Hannah, 10, from her marriage to Griffin Dunne), was grateful, nonetheless, for the presence of real doctors.

F AMILY MATTERS

Well, all righty, then. *Fargo* star William H. Macy, 50, and wife Felicity Huffman, 37, of TV's *Sports Night,* became first-time parents on August 1, when daughter Sofia Grace was born.

"I think she's incredibly spoiled," said Madonna affectionately of daughter Lourdes, 3. On August 10, Lola, as she is called, got a rival when half brother Rocco Ritchie arrived. Madonna, just six days shy of her 42nd birthday, had an emergency caesarean-section delivery at Los Angeles's Cedars-Sinai Medical Center. Dad is her English director beau, Guy Ritchie, 31.

Now master of her parents' domain, Sascha Seinfeld arrived in New York City on Election Day. Her folks are Jerry, 46, a onetime sitcom star, and Jessica, 29, a public relations exec.

Cheryl Tiegs, 52, and yoga-master husband Rod Stryker, 42, used a surrogate to carry their twin boys, Theo and Jaden, explaining it all to Tiegs's son Zach, 8, this way: "Mommy couldn't grow them in her tummy." The boy replied, "What is it? A plant?"

Olympian Michael Johnson has run the 400 in 43.18, but his son Sebastian made Johnson, 32, and wife Kerry, 37, parents in an instant on May 6.

"Look at that dimple!" said Catherine Zeta-Jones, 30, of her newborn son Dylan, whose face takes after Dad, Michael Douglas, 55, and grandpa Kirk. Four months later, the couple tied a ribbon around it, getting married in Manhattan.

Titanic's Kate Winslet, 25, and husband Jim Threapleton, 26, a director, got a second-anniversary present six weeks early when Mia was born October 12.

From Costars to Lovers

Meg Ryan falls for Russell Crowe and divorces Dennis Quaid

On location far away from home and working in close quarters, Meg Ryan fell in love with her romantic lead. The year was 1988, the film was *D.O.A.,* and her costar was Dennis Quaid. After sticking by him as he battled drug addiction, she married Quaid, and in 1992 the couple had a son, Jack. They put Jack before their careers, turning down film roles that would take them both away from home at the same time. This past year Ryan, 38, took a part in *Proof of Life*. In it, Russell Crowe, 36, the Australian man-of-the-moment and star of last summer's *Gladiator,* would play a hostage crisis negotiator who tries to free Ryan's husband and becomes involved with her.

The film was shot in Ecuador, where Ryan found herself once again falling in love with her romantic lead. Between shots, reported a staffer at the hotel where the cast stayed, they were "cuddling, hugging, kissing. Everyone was surprised." Most of all Quaid, said the actor's friends. Later, he and Ryan formally announced their split. She had spent the night before in London, with Crowe, at a David Bowie concert. The day after, Quaid, 46, spoke with his first wife, P.J. Soles, with whom he is still friendly. "I've never heard him sound so sad," she relayed. "I got the feeling he hasn't slept recently." Though Quaid has a reputation for being a flirt on film sets, Soles insists that any bad behavior ended "during the Meg years."

The next month, he and Ryan filed for divorce, agreeing to joint custody of Jack. Eventually Quaid began to date as well. But in August the estranged couple, as ever dedicated to their young son, took him to see *The Nutty Professor II,* and then to church. That they appeared every bit the family might explain why some friends met the actors' initial separation by saying, "I'm flabbergasted."

Quaid and Ryan, said a friend, "adored each other." She added, "You just can't pinpoint the pressures" that broke them up.

Crowe and Ryan filmed for more than a month in South America on *Proof of Life,* then headed to London for some additional scenes.

In the same embroidered tank, Ryan attended the Directors Guild Awards one month later, in March, with Crowe. At the time, the world still thought they were just friends.

SPLIT LEAVES HAN SOLO

They are two of the movies' power players—he gets $25 million a picture, she was the wordsmith behind *E.T.*—and their marriage was thought to be the industry gold standard. Homesteading with their two kids in Jackson Hole, Wyoming, Harrison Ford, 58, and Melissa Mathison, 50, had been wed 17 years when they suddenly revealed that they were living apart. "We sincerely hope that we can work out our differences," said an announcement possibly aimed at deflecting rumors of any infidelity. Famously private, Ford has offered little insight into his family life over the years. He did, however, allow in a 1998 interview that "it's on the set where I feel the most valued. I'm probably a better actor than I am a father or husband."

"While we continue to be committed to the long-term success of our marriage," said the press release on the trial separation of Ted Turner, 61, and Jane Fonda, 62, "we find ourselves at a juncture where we must each take some personal time."

When 17-year-olds Macauley Culkin and Rachel Miner wed in June 1998, cynics said it wouldn't last. Well, it didn't. The actors split in August, announcing through Culkin's spokesman that they "remain the best of friends."

"Scary Spice" Melanie Brown, 24, divorced her husband of 16 months, former Spice Girls tour dancer Jimmy Gulzar, 32. The pair have an 11-month-old daughter, Phoenix Chi.

A couple for five years, *Mad About You* actors Hank Azaria, 36, and Helen Hunt, 37, postponed their honeymoon due to film commitments and then split after several months of wedlock.

Two days after they danced together at a White House dinner, Melissa Etheridge (near right), 39, and partner Julie Cypher, 36, announced they were separating "with the utmost love and respect for one another." The couple will share custody of their two children, raising them together in side-by-side houses with a common backyard.

Accepting an American Music Award last January, Garth Brooks, 37, told wife Sandy, 35, and 10 million viewers, "We don't know what's going to happen." What eventually happened was that, after 14 years together and one separation, they again parted.

Overexposed clothing designer Tommy Hilfiger, 49, and his wife Susie, 41, called it quits after two decades and four children together. She reportedly stayed in their Connecticut estate, and he bought one of his own across the street.

"I'm glad it doesn't appear that plates have been hurling around the kitchen," said a friend of Elizabeth Hurley, 34, and her live-in love of 13 years, Hugh Grant, 39. The on-and-off-again pair said their separation was "a mutual and amicable decision."

Ellen DeGeneres, 42, and Anne Heche, 31, who wore matching wedding bands and called each other "wife," suddenly parted after 3½ years. Heche was subsequently seen with Coley Laffoon, a cameraman on her documentary about DeGeneres's 2000 comedy tour.

Country star Naomi Judd, 54, would not tolerate the cheating heart of husband Larry Strickland, 54, and, after 11 years, filed for divorce. Strickland had managed the career of Judd's singing daughter, Wynonna.

Side by side last year when they disclosed that he has multiple sclerosis, Montel Williams, 43, and wife Grace, 36, seemed closer than ever. Just months later they split, saying they would share custody of their two kids.

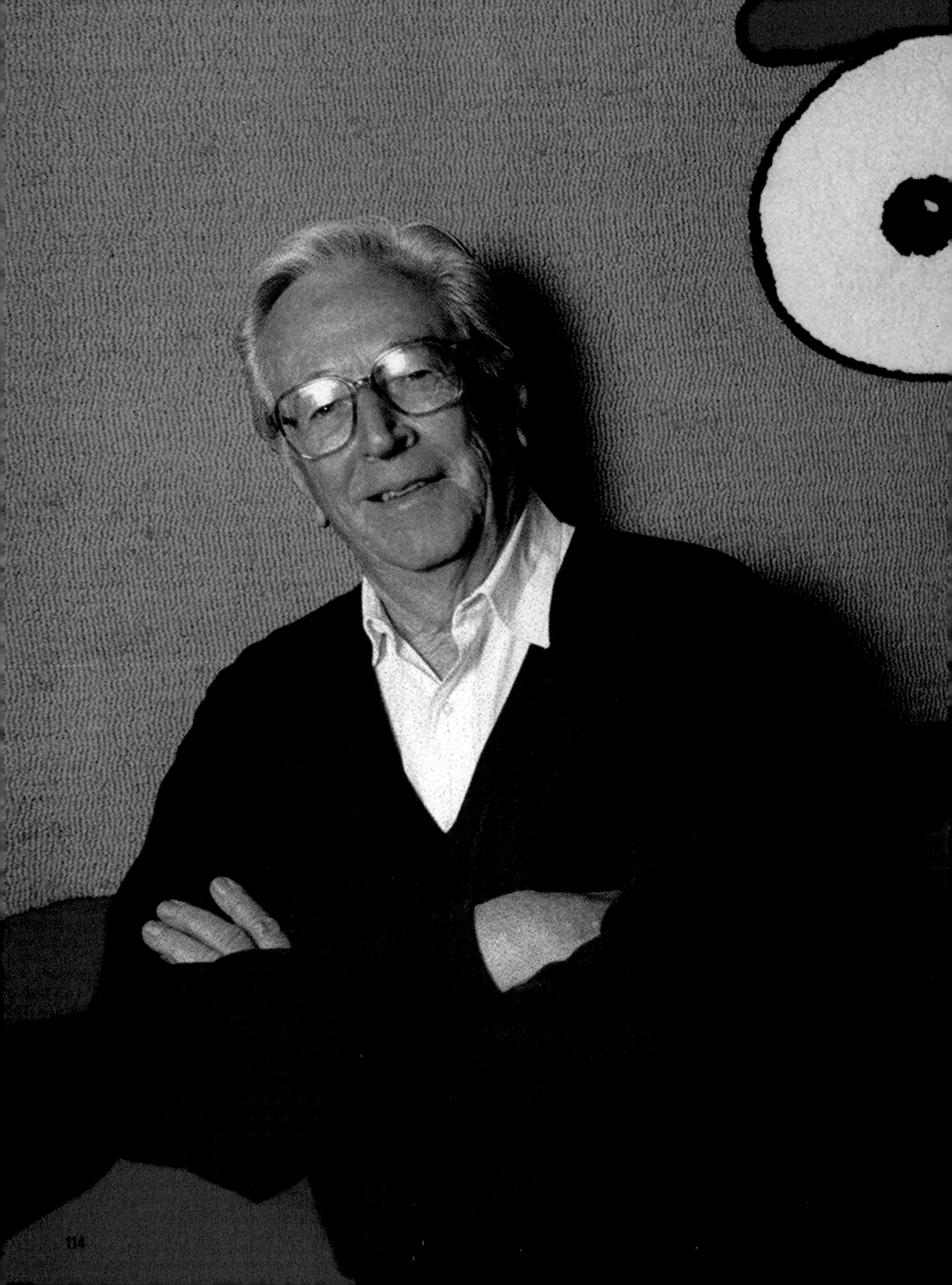

Drawing on his own insecurities, which were anything but *Peanuts*-size, he tickled the fiendish inner child in us all

CHARLES M. SCHULZ

The beloved comic strip that made us feel better about the woeful side of ourselves served a similar purpose for its creator. "He used the strip as therapy," said *Hagar the Horrible* comic-strip artist Chris Browne. "He reached into the muck of his own soul and came up with diamonds."

For nearly 50 years, Charles M. Schulz so sparklingly sprinkled those diamonds that they came to epitomize American culture at its most innocent and touching. Along the way, they were read daily in 75 countries and even were exhibited—"Good grief!"—in the Louvre. "All his life he just wanted to be witty and carefree like Snoopy," says Amy Lago, Schulz's editor at United Media, "but despite all the success, he still felt like Charlie Brown."

Charles Monroe Schulz grew up in St. Paul, the only child of Carl, a barber, and his wife, Dena. A shy, skinny teenager with a bad complexion, he flunked algebra, physics, English and Latin. He yearned to be a cartoonist and practiced by drawing Popeye. When he was 15, *Ripley's Believe It or Not!* accepted a drawing of his dog Spike. Yet the cartoons Schulz submitted for his high school yearbook were rejected. "I was a bland, stupid-looking kid who started off badly and failed everything," he said.

Perhaps from such self-doubt sprang his own acute sensitivity to the melodramas of childhood—and to the needs of his own five children. Though his first marriage ended in divorce (he married again in 1974), Schulz proved a lasting success as a father. "If I had to sum up my feelings about Dad, it would be this," says his son Craig, 47. "He was the finest example of a human being I ever met."

"A lot of the strips stemmed from what we were doing at one time or another," recalls son Craig (second from right, with sibs Jill, Amy, Monte, their mother Joyce and Dad in 1965). Below, left: Schulz with early versions of his *Peanuts* pals.

The aspiring cartoonist took an art correspondence course, but before he could embark on a career he was drafted into the Army during World War II. He left for boot camp only days after his mother died of cancer; the loss and loneliness, he said, scarred him for life. After the war, working as an art instructor at the Minneapolis correspondence school where he had once enrolled, he fell in love with a beautiful auburn-haired coworker in accounting, Donna Johnson. Schulz proposed after a long courtship, but Johnson turned him down to marry a fireman. "It's a blow to everything that you are. Your appearance. Your personality," he told a friend. Johnson was later immortalized as the Little Red-Haired Girl who continually breaks Charlie Brown's heart.

In 1949 Schulz married Joyce Halverson, and they had five children. After 23 years, his marriage ended. "I don't think she liked me anymore, and I just got up and left one day," he explained. A year later Schulz, who was a teetotaler and a Sunday school teacher, met and married Jeannie Clyde.

Peanuts, originally called *Li'l Folks,* debuted in seven newspapers on Oct. 2, 1950, earning Schulz $90 a week in royalties. The cartoonist broke ground by depicting love, hope, pain and loss—with humor and compassion. "There used to be so many taboo things in cartoons, and he blasted that to smithereens," says Schulz's biographer Rheta Grimsley Johnson. Eventually *Peanuts* brought its author $30 to $40 million annually, much of it from merchandise and product endorsements.

Schulz died of colon cancer at 77, the very night before the last original *Peanuts* strip was to run in Sunday papers. To his fans he left a legacy of smiles and self-recognition. He had once said of *Peanuts,* "All the loves in the strip are unrequited; all the baseball games are lost; all the test scores are D-minuses; the Great Pumpkin never comes; and the football is always pulled away." Only Schulz could make us see the humor in that.

CHAS. M. SCHULZ
2162 COFFEE LANE

SIR JOHN GIELGUD

His mellifluous voice suited Macbeth, Hamlet, Oberon and one bratty butler

Though theater was in his blood—his grandmother, "great-aunt" and cousin were actors—this son of a London stockbroker father had to promise his folks that if he didn't establish a stage career by age 25, he would give up that dream for their preference, architecture. Already as a teenager, he did walk-ons at the Old Vic. But his early speaking roles were not encouraging, and critics were lukewarm about his first Romeo. He continued to pay his dues, however, and earned leads in *Richard II, Macbeth* and *A Midsummer Night's Dream*. Then, at age 25—his deadline for success—came Hamlet. "The high water mark of English Shakespearean acting in our time," wrote one reviewer, and Britain would have to do with one less architect. Over the next seven decades, Gielgud (who was knighted in 1953) could count on those sorts of notices, whether on the West End or in TV's *Brideshead Revisited.* "Fortunately, I've had very good friends who have been critical of me," he told *The New York Times,* just before his 90th birthday. "They haven't flattered me too much so that I acquired a sense of my own importance. That's a danger for an actor." Surprisingly, he won his only Oscar as the starched yet vulgar butler in 1981's *Arthur* (above, with Dudley Moore). If Gielgud was perfection onstage, in life he was known for his social gaffes. "Didn't Richard [Burton] marry some terrible film star?" he blithely inquired of Elizabeth Taylor. Never retired (he appeared in 1998's *Elizabeth* with Cate Blanchett), Gielgud lived in a Brideshead-like estate in Buckinghamshire and died a year after his longtime partner, Martin Hensler, at 96.

RICHARD **MULLIGAN**

A serial husband in life, he fathered
two unconventional TV families

A Bronx boy who once contemplated the priesthood,
Richard Mulligan was launched by his director big brother
Robert Mulligan with a bit part in *Love with the Proper
Stranger* and followed up playing General Custer in *Little
Big Man.* After more films and a turn on Broadway, he
became the bemused patriarch on the breakthrough TV
comedy *Soap.* That role, and that of the widowed dad
(left, with dog Dreyfuss) in the sitcom *Empty Nest,* won
him two Emmys. His private life was less rewarding.
Divorced four times, he was alone when he died, at 67, of
cancer. His son James remembers his dad's hard-won
advice: "Do well with your life, find a nice person to be
with, have a family and do work you enjoy."

WALTER **MATTHAU**

The 'Ukrainian Cary Grant' slunk into our hearts with unrivaled rumpled charm

His wrinkled-bedsheet face and gruff tone made him an unlikely romantic lead. Yet 1969's *Cactus Flower* saw him utterly convincing as the object of both Ingrid Bergman's and Goldie Hawn's affections. This was the Walter Matthau paradox: He made slouchy sexy. Born Walter Matuschanskayasky to Jewish immigrant parents, he was raised by his seamstress mother, Rose, after his father abandoned the family. A child of the Depression, he earned extra money selling ice cream outside the Yiddish theaters of New York's Lower East Side. By age 11, he had a small part in a play. After high school he coached boxing and worked for the Montana forest service, before entering the Army. For three years he was a radio operator and cryptographer in London. The G.I. Bill paid for a theater degree back in New York. Soon he was known, not as a star, but as a dependable actor if you needed a villain or the guy next door. That was until a 1965 breakout Broadway performance as Oscar Madison in *The Odd Couple*. He re-created the part on film opposite Jack Lemmon, eventually his 10-time collaborator. The role cemented Matthau's image as a cantankerous slob. In fact, he was a joyful man who loved Mozart and horse races second only to family. His first marriage ended after a decade in 1958; his second, to Carol Marcus, spanned 41 years until his death at 79, from a heart attack. Charlie, the youngest of his three children, directed some of his dad's later films. Carol Burnett remembers Matthau kissing Charlie on the set each morning: "Walter would go, 'Moochie moochie moochie,' and pinch his son's cheeks and look at me and say, 'Isn't he delicious?' He just knew how to love."

NANCY **MARCHAND**

She built a career by playing patrician ladies but, *mamma mia,* what a finale

"I love to act!" Nancy Marchand once said. She drew it out: "I *loooove* . . ." She loved the challenge, though directors often asked her to stick with Waspy characters that could have been plucked from her own Upstate New York family tree. The best known in her gallery of prim portrayals was Mrs. Pynchon, the neatly coiffed publisher on *Lou Grant*. But at the end of her life, fighting cancer and sometimes wheeling an oxygen tank behind her, Marchand finally got a big, earthy, nothing-like-her role. With gleeful ease she became *The Sopranos'* mob matriarch Livia, a mother who orders a hit on her son for putting her in a nursing home. "That woman," said Marchand, who died at 71, "was a hoot!"

HEDY LAMARR

Vienna spawned a mother of seduction—and invention

"Any girl can look glamorous," Hedy Lamarr once remarked. "All you have to do is stand still and look stupid." For Lamarr, playing dumb was a stretch. In 1942 she and composer friend George Antheil patented an antijamming method for radio signals that, in refined form, was later deployed in missile-guidance and cell-phone technology. (When, in 1997, she and Antheil were honored for their work, Lamarr said, "It's about time.") But Lamarr, a banker's daughter born Hedwig Eva Marie Kiesler in Vienna, was best known for her skinny-dipping scene in the oft-banned 1933 Czech film *Ecstasy* and for Hollywood credits like *Algiers, Boom Town* and *Samson and Delilah.* Wed six times and notoriously difficult and litigious, she turned down the Ingrid Bergman roles in *Casablanca* and *Gaslight* and sued Mel Brooks for mocking her name in *Blazing Saddles.* When she died at 85 in Orlando, she was legally blind but still, recalled one of her three children, "totally hip and chic."

DOUGLAS FAIRBANKS JR.

A gentleman actor preferred diplomacy to stardom

Born of Hollywood royalty, Douglas Fairbanks Jr. emerged from his father's swash-buckling shadow to become an actor, highly decorated naval officer and goodwill ambassador. As historian Arthur Schlesinger Jr. observed before Fairbanks died, at 90, of Parkinson's disease, "He stood for gallantry in a notably ungallant time."

"I never tried to compete with him," the suave Fairbanks Jr. said of his silent-film-star dad. "To start with, he was the most physically agile person I knew. He could climb anything." Young Douglas began his own rise in New York City and lived with his mother, Anna Beth Sully, after his father divorced her to marry Mary Pickford. He made his acting debut at 13 and struggled to support his mom variously as a prop man, cameraman and writer of silent film titles. Eventually, he played in nearly 80 films, including *Gunga Din* and *The Corsican Brothers* (right), but none gained as much attention as did his four-year marriage to Joan Crawford (the first of his three wives). An Anglophile and fervent backer of FDR, Fairbanks was sent by the President on an intelligence and support-building mission to South America in 1941. Later he saw combat leading a British flotilla in the North Atlantic. After the war he hosted and acted in a popular TV anthology series but preferred working behind the camera and entertaining at his London home. "I became aware that I could never be a creative actor," he said. "I prefer being a fly on the wall in the corridors of power."

PATRICK O'BRIAN

A master maritime novelist captured the Napoleonic era from an Elba of his own

Although he penned 20 immensely popular novels chronicling the exploits of the British navy during the Napoleonic Wars and was compared to Melville and Conrad, Patrick O'Brian's greatest creation might have been himself. His series—which featured British naval officer Jack Aubrey and Stephen Maturin, an Irish-Catalan physician, naturalist and spy—sold more than 2 million copies, despite the author's having fled publicity and the world to live in a French fishing village. O'Brian, who died at 85, claimed to have been a sickly child schooled at his Galway home, but he was in fact born Richard Patrick Russ in London to a physician of German descent and an English mother. O'Brian's second marriage, to an English divorcée, lasted four decades. His legacy included two CDs of the music Aubrey and Maturin played at sea, as well as a recipe book for dishes eaten aboard the *H.M.S. Surprise,* including several for rat.

DON BUDGE

Wham! Bam! He won the first Grand Slam

Trained as a teenager on the gridiron and the soccer field, Californian Don Budge brought a revolutionary aggressive style and a devastating rolling backhand to the once patty-cake game of tennis. Rangy (6'2"), burly and with flaming red hair, he completed the sport's first Grand Slam in 1938, having won the Australian, U.S. and French Opens as well as Wimbledon (right). The year before, he led the Americans to a Davis Cup victory over a German team (which had received an exhortative phone call from Hitler); his clinching match, played in London, was witnessed by Jack Benny and Queen Mary. Budge later turned pro (the Opens and the Cup were for amateurs only then), retired in 1953 and died at 84 from injuries incurred in a car accident.

HAROLD NICHOLAS

Dancing feats took him from vaudeville to film

Tapping since age 5 on Philadelphia's black vaudeville stages, Harold Nicholas and big brother Fayard redefined the genre as an athletic, balletic, whole-body medium. Discovered at New York City's Cotton Club by Sam Goldwyn, they would appear in nearly 60 films in as many years (including 1988's *Tap,* left). In the earliest releases, the Nicholas Brothers' dance sequences were often edited out by distributors in the South. Nicholas, who died at 79 of heart failure, was married first to star-crossed actress Dorothy Dandridge, then to Rigmor Newman, mother of his two children.

CRAIG **C**LAIBORNE

A mouth from the South boosted worldly cuisine

"Many's the night I've lain in bed worrying about the stellar worth of one restaurant or another, about whether I was justified in referring to a chef's Mornay sauce as mucilage." These are the sleep-depriving concerns of only a dedicated food writer. A Navy officer during the Korean War and then a put-upon PR man in Chicago, Craig Claiborne willingly shouldered the burden of his influential role as food editor of *The New York Times*. The job, until Claiborne grabbed it in 1957, had always been held by a woman. But it fit the Mississippi-raised, Swiss-trained chef like a bespoke toque. "All my life I'd been miserable, anxious and frightened," he once admitted. "Now I have everything. All I want is for it to continue." It did, for a fruitful 29 years. In addition, Claiborne (below, on his 50th birthday), along with colleague Pierre Franey, penned several cookbooks, including one dedicated to the catfish and corn bread of his mother's Southern kitchen. Mostly, though, he aimed to liberate Americans' constrained palates, encouraging them to try fine French and authentic Asian cuisine. Fans followed him loyally, save for the time when he wrote about a dinner in Paris he had won in an auction. The 1975 meal, shared with Franey, consisted of 31 courses and cost $4,000. In droves, readers wrote in expressing disgust. Claiborne, who died at 79, maintained a critic's detachment, pronouncing the lobster "chewy" and the oysters "lukewarm."

Barbara Cartland
Her plots made Di's step-grandma co–queen of hearts

In terms of output, she made Stephen King look like a slacker. No fewer than 723 demurely chaste romance novels sprang from the mind of Dame Barbara Cartland, who was likely dreaming up the next when she died in her sleep at 98. The English author's first effort, *Jigsaw,* came out in 1921, and in the next seven decades she saw more than a billion copies of her work in print. Preferring to dictate to assistants, she rarely touched a typewriter (keeping her hands free for pals like Twi-Twi, above). She was already a success with fans, if not critics, when she married Alexander McCorquodale in 1927, and their daughter Raine grew up to be Princess Diana's stepmother. After six years the couple split bitterly. But, as in her novels, the heroine found love in the end, wedding her ex's cousin Hugh. That union produced two sons and lasted until his death in 1963.

SIR ALEC **GUINNESS**
In the Old Vic or a galaxy far, far away, he was a master

"Not the acting type," declared his boarding school headmaster. "Never make actor," sneered a drama coach who dropped him. But young Alec Guinness didn't listen, a fact less meaningful had he not distinguished himself as an actor who listened. Where others thundered through their pages, Guinness held back, pondered and reacted. That subtle difference was not lost on John Gielgud, who gave him a bit part in a 1934 *Hamlet* and in a work about Noah's Ark which introduced Guinness to his wife, Merula Salaman, who played a fellow animal. By 24 the London native had made Hamlet his own, and was on his way to a 1959 knighthood. After serving in the Royal Navy he took on film. *Great Expectations* began a collaboration with David Lean, who directed him to an Oscar in *The Bridge on the River Kwai.* Made for the close-up, his malleable face became an Arab prince (*Lawrence of Arabia*), a Japanese businessman (*A Majority of One*) and an entire family (*Kind Hearts and Coronets*). Younger audiences knew it best peering out of a brown hooded cloak as Obi-Wan Kenobi; *Star Wars* earned Guinness a bigger paycheck than all the others combined. Still, dinners out with his wife were his only extravagance, and he continued to work until he lost his fight with cancer at 86.

ROGER VADIM

God created woman . . .
one man gave thanks on film

Roger Vadim held on to his male friends, it was said, because he didn't gloat. He once described a nap à trois with Brigitte Bardot and Ursula Andress, a pal notes, but "didn't say it boastfully." A French diplomat's son, he made BB a sex symbol with his debut film, *And God Created Woman.* They wed when she turned 18. His second wife and mother of his first child was Annette Stroyberg (*Les Liaisons Dangereuses*). Later amour Catherine Deneuve (*Vice and Virtue*) gave him a son. Vadim then married Jane Fonda (right, star of his *Barbarella*); they had a daughter. Wife No. 4, actress Catherine Schneider, mothered a fourth child. Taken by cancer at 72, Vadim is survived by his fifth wife, actress Marie-Christine Barrault. Critics dispute the weight of his work, but, noted French president Jacques Chirac, "he knew how to create myths."

DAVID MERRICK

Talent, plus ruthlessness, made
him the 'Abominable Showman'

If she ever needed a heart transplant, Phyllis Diller wanted David Merrick's because, she said, "it's never been used." What he lacked in human warmth, the oft-married and divorced stage producer made up with love for the theater. A shopkeeper's son from St. Louis, he gave up law to pursue his passion in New York City. His first hit was 1954's *Fanny.* At one point in 1958, the lights of four Broadway theaters beaconed Merrick productions. Along the way he gave a leg up to the careers of Ethel Merman, Carol Channing and Barbra Streisand. While Merrick loved the glitzy spectacle of *Gypsy* or *Hello, Dolly,* he also showcased the cutting pens of Tom Stoppard and John Osborne. And he was a master of promotion: During a curtain call of *42nd Street* he announced the death of its director, Gower Champion, just to grab publicity. The last of the 10-time Tony winner's 80 shows was a 1996 *State Fair* revival. "No one," said critic Frank Rich of Merrick, who died at 88, "had a record like his."

JIM **VARNEY**

The comic never underestimated the importance of being Ernest

It should have been a onetime thing. Sell cars for a local Tennessee dealer by appearing in a TV ad as a gratingly lovable hick who repeatedly asked a never-seen foil named Vern, "Know what I mean?" But the character, Ernest P. Worrell, outran his creator, Jim Varney. A comedian who once performed Shakespeare, Varney voiced Slinky Dog in *Toy Story* and its sequel, and scored sitcom walk-ons. But Ernest headlined nine works for film and TV. Both were lost when cancer took the actor at age 50.

STEVE **REEVES**

Before the 'Muscles from Brussels,'
there was the 'Chest from the West'

As a puny kid in Oakland, Steve Reeves began lifting weights after losing an arm-wrestling match to a yet smaller boy. Bodybuilding became his passion, and in the late 1940s he took several titles, including Mr. Universe. Hollywood rang, but Reeves turned down offers from Cecil B. DeMille that required him to drop some bulk. Instead, he opted for an Italian producer who made him the title star of 18 successful, if critically laughed off, Hercules flicks. By the time he retired in 1969, Reeves, who died at 74 of lymphoma, had paved a career path for such jocks-turned-thespians as Arnold Schwarzenegger and Belgian Jean-Claude Van Damme.

DOUG **HENNING**

Doing magic in the tie-dye era, he
made the timeworn tuxedo vanish

"Have Rabbit, Will Travel." When the Ontario teen placed the ad, he couldn't guess how far it would take him. In the 1970s Doug Henning was a fixture on Broadway, in Vegas and on TV, with his bell-bottom cool spin on classic tricks like Harry Houdini's "Metamorphosis," in which he trapped a handcuffed assistant in a sack within a padlocked chest, and then traded places with her in less than 10 seconds. (Houdini took 20.) In the 1980s he dedicated himself to transcendental meditation, and before he died of cancer at 52, he was planning a spiritual theme park.

GEORGE SEGAL

Using people and plaster as his medium, he made realism more real

As a painter supporting himself by teaching art in the 1950s, George Segal, who died at 75, received career-transforming inspiration when a student brought him the medical scrim used for orthopedic casts. He asked his wife, Helen, to wrap him head-to-toe. Then he cast others, transforming their human poses into works reminiscent of heroic Greek sculpture. A 1962 show put him into the pop-art pantheon alongside the likes of Claes Oldenburg, and allowed him to stop teaching. By placing his plaster, and later bronze, people in settings, he created social dioramas. *Fireside Chat* honored FDR; *Gay Liberation* stands at the site of a Greenwich Village uprising. Never comfortable calling himself a sculptor, Segal instead likened his techniques of precise replication to photography.

ADMIRAL ELMO ZUMWALT

A Navy reformer paid dearly for an order he gave in Vietnam

Though he opposed expanded U.S. involvement in Vietnam, Adm. Elmo Zumwalt Jr. was entrusted with overseeing naval forces in the Mekong Delta. His strategy included use of the defoliant Agent Orange to uncover snipers in the jungle. Years later, when veterans charged that the chemical caused cancer and other ills in themselves and their children, the admiral's son was among them. Lt. Elmo Zumwalt III, who had commanded a ship in the region, developed lymphoma, and his own son suffered a profound learning disability. After the war Zumwalt issued directives, called Z-Grams, to encourage promotion of minorities and women in the Navy. But with his son's illness and death in 1988, he focused on aiding veterans and establishing the first national bone marrow donor program. Zumwalt died at 79 after surgery for a tumor. "I still would have ordered the defoliation to achieve the objectives it did," he wrote in 1986. "But that does not ease the sorrow I feel."

EDWARD GOREY

The aptly named artist and poet inked a comically ghastly world

"A is for Amy, who fell down the stairs . . ." So begins a ghoulish alphabet cheerfully enumerating how 26 pale, ill-fated youths meet their demise. The humor, and the intricate line drawings of forlorn figures in foreboding Victorian settings, are unmistakably Edward Gorey. The author and illustrator of more than 100 books (including *The Irontonic,* right) succumbed to a heart attack at 75. He lived with several cats, in a house plagued by poison ivy. But Gorey's life was far less gloomy than his art suggests. He loved Matisse and the ballet, and a covey of many, many friends. A theater buff, he designed sets and collaborated on musicals of his own stories. TV viewers saw his stylish animation in the credits of *Mystery.* The segment featured a fatal piece of garden statuary.

John Cardinal O'Connor

The Pope's envoy in New York blended doctrine with compassion

His predecessor at the New York Archdiocese, Terence Cardinal Cooke, called himself a "a simple parish priest." When John Cardinal O'Connor was tapped by Pope John Paul II to head the nation's most visible Catholic pulpit, he said, "I'm a priest. How simple I don't know." "Not very" was the message of his 16-year reign. Soft-spoken, with no taste for fire-and-brimstone sermons, he nonetheless followed services with a press conference, and his sound-bite moral lessons often hit the front page of the tabloids. His unwavering defense of Church teachings on abortion, homosexuality and women's ordination put him at odds with local liberal politics. But even as he opposed equality for gays, he ministered in AIDS wards. And though he once stirred controversy by comparing abortions to the killing of Jews in the Holocaust, he preached against anti-Semitism and racism. A Philadelphian who spent 27 years as a military chaplain serving in Korea and Vietnam, O'Connor became as much a part of New York City as its resplendent St. Patrick's Cathedral. He died in his residence, at 80, from cancer.

Gwen Verdon

Her ties with Bob Fosse gave legs to Lola, Charity and Roxie

Having traded in corrective shoes for tap shoes as a child, Gwen Verdon was 28—all but over-the-hill for a hoofer—when she hit Broadway in 1953 in *Can Can*. The redhead stole the show and won her first Tony. On her follow-up, *Damn Yankees* (right, as Lola, with Stephen Douglas), she met choreographer Bob Fosse, with whom she would enjoy an intensely productive professional relationship (earning three more Tonys in his musicals *Yankees, Sweet Charity* and *Chicago*) as well as a turbulent marriage. Wed in 1960, they had a daughter, Nicole (Verdon already had a son, James), and separated in 1971 after Fosse's numerous flings. They never divorced, nor let their failed romance affect their collaboration—she even worked with and befriended Fosse's lover before his 1987 death, Ann Reinking. After appearing in films (*Cocoon, The Cotton Club*), Verdon returned to the boards a year before her death at 75 as artistic director of *Fosse,* a 1999 anthology that captured for posterity her sensual movement and his iconic, jazz-imbued choreography.

STEVE ALLEN
The godfather of late-night was a renaissance showman

The formula is so familiar, it seems rooted in nature rather than one maestro's imagination: Music from a live band. A man comes out, tells a few jokes, sits down to banter with a celeb. Then a little humorous shtick, another interview, and 'night, folks, see you tomorrow. Before Paar, Carson, Leno or Letterman, there was Steve Allen, the son of vaudevillians and a popular radio deejay. From 1954 to 1957 he ran *Tonight,* where his Question Man inspired Carnac, and escapades like diving into a vat of Jell-O were ur-Stupid Human Tricks. He hosted PBS's *Meeting of the Minds* in the '70s and later chaired the Parents Television Council, seeking to censor vulgar sexual content. Married twice, he and second wife Jayne Meadows often teamed on behalf of the disenfranchised, from migrant workers to Afghan women. In between, Allen, who died at 78 after a heart attack, found time to write 53 books and thousands of songs—including "This Could Be the Start of Something (Big)"—earning him a Guinness record as the most prolific contemporary composer.

JEAN-PIERRE RAMPAL

A virtuoso piper turned his 14-karat gold flute into a musical magic wand

French flutist Jean-Pierre Rampal cut through the classical music world with a rock star's charisma, his albums lasting like Pink Floyd's up to 10 years on the charts. At 6'1", he was a looming stage presence in a genre that previously had saved celebrity for an elite group of pianists and string soloists. His mother preferred that her boy become a doctor, but his father, a flutist with the Marseilles symphony, started him on the instrument. Eventually, when the war forced his relocation to Paris, Rampal left medical school, and in 1945 he joined the orchestra of the Paris Opera. Soon after, he married harpist Françoise Bacqueyrisse, with whom he had two children, and began a parallel career as a solo recitalist and recording artist. Favoring Bach and Vivaldi, Rampal (above, with pianist Georges Solchany in 1968) also ventured into Japanese folk music and American rag. In any category, his technique was impeccable. As one critic put it, "The Rampal tone is firm, rounded, richly varied within the natural scope of the instrument's capabilities, which, in fact, Rampal has redefined and expanded." He was a maestro also of promotion. Playing his gold flute to massive audiences until his heart failed at 78, he once admitted, "We are all a little ham, you know."

TITO PUENTE

Headlining 300 shows a year till the end, the Mambo King played songs to love

In the New York City barrio where bandleader Tito Puente was born, they still call him *El Rey*—The King. Last year, as Latin popsters like Ricky Martin and Enrique Iglesias broke through, Puente began the sixth decade of a career launched when he and his *timbales* (below, in 1998) brought the enchanting rhythms of Latin jazz to swing clubs. And he was prepared to keep banging away: Not long before his heart gave out at age 77, Puente was still rousing crowds worldwide with hits like "Oye Como Va" and others from his 118 albums. The son of Puerto Rican immigrants, Puente began drumming the day he could pick up a spoon and his mother's pots. Save for a stint in the Navy during World War II (which helped pay for a Juilliard education), he never stopped. In the 1992 film *The Mambo Kings,* Puente energetically and convincingly portrayed himself in the 1950s club scene. "I have not taken a vacation in my whole life," he said in 2000. "You know when you're on vacation? When the phone don't ring."

BIG **PUN**

Real-world rhymes made him Latino hip-hop's biggest star

Where many rappers limit themselves to gangsta topics like sex and crime, Big Pun (for "Punisher") saw all of life as material. "Losing your job, losing a loved one, stress, happiness, whatever," he said. He distinguished himself with his "sophisticated hardcore" style, and, as the leading Latino rap artist, infusing his mixes with salsa. Born Christopher Rios to Puerto Rican parents in New York City, he was an athlete in his svelter high school days. At over 600 pounds, Big Pun's weight didn't make him any less loved by fans. But it did cost this husband and father of three his life, when his heart failed at 28.

MAURICE RICHARD

In the ice wars of the NHL, the most
lethal weapon ever was the Rocket

Goalies likened his approach to the terror of a car coming
at you at night. His stick was an assault weapon. His
combination of brute intimidation and shooting preci-
sion made Maurice "Rocket" Richard arguably hockey's
greatest superstar and led his Canadiens to eight Stanley
Cups. Centering his line was his brother Henri, who was
known as the Pocket Rocket and joined him in the Hall
of Fame. Maurice's talent was matched by his temper.
He punched or choked errant refs, and his native
Montreal exploded in the "Richard Riot" when the
league suspended him in 1955. Before Richard's death
from stomach cancer and Parkinson's disease at 78, the
NHL established the Richard trophy for the season's
high goal scorer. The Rocket would have earned five.

TOM LANDRY

Stoic on the sidelines, the man
in the hat had a head to win

He wasn't the NFL coach with the best record.
(Don Shula and George Halas outrank him.)
But, as Cowboy Danny White put it, Tom Landry
"cared about the players far more than wins and
losses"—and rarely lost. A native of Mission,
Texas, he flew in combat in World War II before
playing defensive back in the pros. As a coach,
he steered the Dallas franchise from its birth in
1960 into five Super Bowls, two championships
and 20 consecutive winning seasons. Near
emotionless on the job, he surprised the sports
world by weeping publicly after his 1989
dismissal. Landry, who died at 75 from leukemia,
retired rather than coach another team.

Pierre Trudeau

A taste for fast cars and glittery women belied this leader's influential intellect

History books might remember Pierre Elliott Trudeau as a visionary prime minister who, from 1968 to 1984, held Canada together with his powerful argument for unity, virtually ended separatist terrorism in his native Quebec and persuaded Britain to let his country write its own constitution. But those who lived through Trudeau's high-flying years will also have racier memories. That trademark rose boutonniere. The seemingly impromptu (but in fact planned) pirouette in a Buckingham Palace hallway. The first wife, Margaret, 29 years his junior, who took off after six years of marriage to photograph rock bands. (Trudeau kept custody of their three sons.) The liaisons with Barbra Streisand and Margot Kidder. Most of all, a swelling of Canadian pride and prestige that centered on one man's leadership and charisma known as Trudeaumania. Among his few detractors were Americans who frowned on his welcoming U.S. draft dodgers, and Ronald Reagan, who found Trudeau's dovelike antinuclear stance naive. After stepping down in 1984, he lived a quiet life and, at 71, had a daughter with lawyer companion Deborah Coyne. Suffering from Parkinson's disease and prostate cancer, he died at 80, a single rose marking his coffin at the state funeral.

Don Martin

His unrivaled wit made the comics go *Shtoink!*

Successfully reducing life to the cells of a comic book takes a sharp eye, a decisive hand and—in the case of Don Martin—a good ear. The world he rendered was noisy, and for three decades in the pages of *Mad* magazine, Martin coined the right words to express its slapstick doings. A brat pulling the wings off a fly? *Glink!* An unsuspecting cheek intercepting a fish? *Spladap!* Brick meets head? *Fwak!* Martin's kinetic drawings of the battle between humans and their stuff gave a signature look to the magazine until the cartoonist quit in 1987 in a feud over free-lancers' rights which ultimately led him to testify before Congress. For a time he penned his strip for the look-alike *Cracked* magazine. And until his death, at 68, of cancer, he defied failing eyesight, pursuing his satiric art holding a magnifying glass.

This anthology of Martin's onomatopoeic masterpieces illustrates why his magazine billed him as "*MAD's* maddest artist."

LORETTA YOUNG

Moviemakers predicted TV would end her bright career, but the canny star proved them wrong

In silent pictures at age 4 and starring in talkies at 15, Loretta Young appeared in 90 films between the 1920s and 1950s. She headlined with Gable, Grant and Tracy, and won an Oscar for *The Farmer's Daughter*. Then, as the industry faced the threat of television, she risked alienating her colleagues by jumping into the new medium. Her *Loretta Young Show* presented a different melodrama each week from 1953 to 1961. It made Young, who died at 87 from cancer, the first actress to win both an Oscar and an Emmy. Notable was her show's opening, in which she twirled in an elegant gown, and its closing, when she delivered the episode's uplifting moral. In 1994, with Young long retired, her adopted daughter, Judy Lewis, wrote that her parents were in fact an unwed Young and Clark Gable, then married to someone else. The adoption, said Lewis, was a cover for what the devoutly Catholic actress knew would have been a scandal.

Screamin' Jay Hawkins

Rhythm-and-blues' resident witch doctor kept his audiences spellbound

"I don't sing them," the former Jalacy J. Hawkins said of his songs. "I destroy them." One of seven children raised by a single mom in Cleveland, he dreamed of a more traditional vocal career and later studied opera at the Ohio Conservatory. But making a buck meant singing in jazz clubs and Fats Domino's band. His breakout began one drunken night when he put a raucous, howling version of the ballad "I Put a Spell on You" on vinyl. Newly minted Screamin' Jay fans loved it. Promoter Alan Freed capitalized on the voodoo image by wheeling him onstage in a zebra-skin-draped coffin. That, and a skull-topped cane named Henry, crystallized a character that Hawkins came to loathe, but was demanded by concertgoers until his death, at 70, after surgery for an aneurysm.

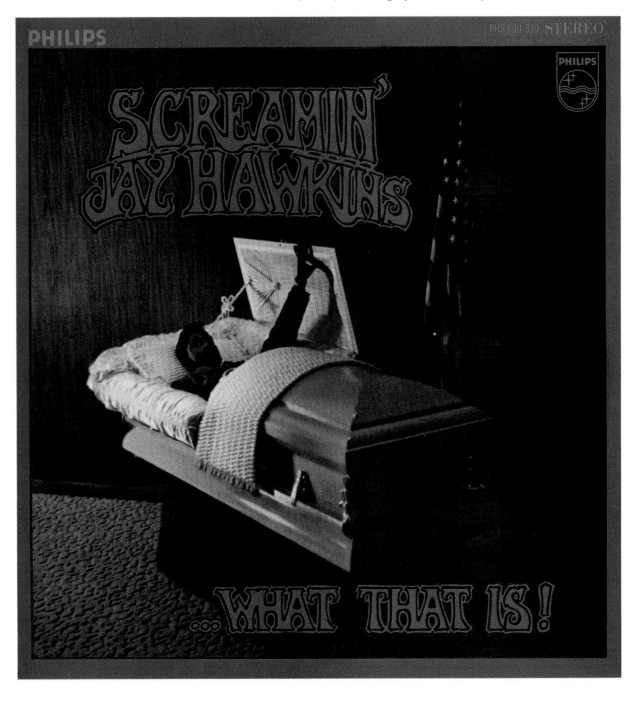

PICTURE CREDITS

FRONT COVER (Aniston and Pitt) Eric Charbonneau/Berliner Studios • (Parker) Online USA • (Woods) Donald Mirelle/Liaison Agency • (Ryan) Evan Agostini/Liaison Agency • (Fox) Luis Martinez/Liaison Agency • (González) Beth Kaiser/AP/WWP • (Hatch) CBS Photo Archive

BACK COVER (Spears and Aguilera) Suzanne Plunkett/AP/WWP • (William) Alpha/Globe Photos • (Tussaud's) Ken Regan/Camera 5

YEAR OF THE SURVIVOR 4-5 (from left) Reuters/Archive; CBS Photo Archive; Christopher Little/Liaison Agency; Doug Mills/AP/WWP; Win McNamee/Reuters/Archive; CBS Photo Archive; Katsumi Kasahara/AP/WWP; Alan Diaz/Reuters/Archive • 6-7 CBS Photo Archive (2) • 8 CBS Photo Archive (4) • 9 (clockwise from top) Theo Westenberger; AP/WWP; Extra; Steve Friedman/Buena Vista; AP/WWP; CBS Photo Archive (3) • 10-11 see on page credits • 12 (top) David J. Phillip/AP/WWP; Ralph Barrera/Austin American-Statesman/AP/WWP • 13 Rick Wilking/Reuters/Archive; Ron Edmonds/AP/WWP • 14-15 (clockwise from top left) Victoria Arocho/AP/WWP; Rene Macura/AP/WPP; Reuters/Archive; Stephan Savoia/AP/WWP; Tami Chappell/Reuters/Archive; Charles Krupa/AP/WWP • 16 Gary M. Prior/Allsport • 17 Robert F. Bukaty/AP/WWP • 18 (from top) Shaun Botterilli/Allsport; Nick Wilson/Allsport; AP/WWP; Reuters/Archive • 19 (from top) Joe McNally; Dan Dockstader/Star Valley Independent; Jeffrey Lowe/Sports Illustrated • 20-21 (clockwise from top left) Univision/AP/WWP; Tony Gutierrez/AP/WWP; Jose Goitia/AP/WWP; Rick Wilking/Reuters/Archive • 22-23 (clockwise from top left) Corbis/Sygma; Pablo Martines Monsivais/AP/WWP; Clark Jones/Impact Visuals; Erik S. Lesser/AP/WWP; Alan Diaz/AP/WWP; Peter Cosgrove/AP/WWP • 24-25 (clockwise from top left) Jim Leynse/SABA; Barbara Nitke/CBS/AP/WWP; John Storey; Mirek Towski/DMI/Timepix

PEOPLE'S PEOPLE 26-27 Corbis/Outline • 28 Alberto Tolot/Corbis/Outline • 29 (from top) Michael O'Neill/Corbis Outline; Robert Sebree • 30-31 Paul Morse/Los Angeles Times/Retna Ltd. • 32 (from top) Armando Gallo/Retna Ltd.; Suzanne Plunkett/AP/WWP • 33 Erica Berger • 34 Mirek Towski/DMI; UK Press; Jim Smeal/Galella Ltd. • 35 Greg DeGuire/London Features; Stephen Trupp/Star Max; Kathy Hutchins/Hutchins Photo Agency • 36 (from top) George Holz; Theo Westenberger • 37 (from left) Stephen Oxenbury/Corbis Outline; Dave Benett/Alpha/Globe Photos • 38 Michael Zeppettello/Icon • 39 (from top) Dana Fineman-Appel/Corbis Sygma; Patrick DeMarchelier/Harper's Bazaar • 40 Jeff Katz • 41 (from top) © Paul Massey/FSP; Jeff Katz

HEADLINERS 42-43 Steve Fenn/ABC; (inset) Marion Curtis/DMI • 44-45 (clockwise from top left) Al Golois/Corbis Sygma; Charles V. Tines/The Detroit News; Linda Rosier; Melissa Lyhle/The Flint Journal/Liaison Agency • 46-47 Tomas Muscionico/Contact Press Images (2) • 48 (from top) Diane Bondareff/AP/WWP; Robert Mecea/AP/WWP • 49 Ann Summa/Liaison Agency; (inset) Carin A. Baer/Fox • 50-51 (clockwise from top) Aleksandar Andjic/AP/WWP; Jake Schoellkopf/AP/WWP; Srdjan Ilic/AP/WWP; Braca Nadezdic/Newsmakers/Liaison Agency • 52 Pierre Roussel/Newsmakers; (inset) Henry McGee/Globe Photos • 53 (from top) Bill Pugliano/Liaison Agency; Andrea Renault/Globe Photos; (inset) Richard Corkery/New York Daily News • 54 Andrea Renault/Globe Photos; (inset) John James/London Features • 55 David Butow/SABA • 56 Jim Smeal/Galella • 57 Jonathan Exley; (inset) Michael Ferguson/Globe Photos • 58 Pat Harbron • 59 Dan Loh/AP/WWP; Nuveen Imagery/AP/WWP • 60 Erica Berger/Corbis Outline; Steve LaBadessa • 61 BCA Films; Greg Brennan • 62 (from top) John Ficara/Corbis Sygma; CNP/MAI; Jim McKnight/AP/WWP • 63 Simon Runting/Rex USA(2)

PARTY ANIMALS 64-65 (from left) Frank Trapper/Corbis Sygma; Mark Terril/AP/WWP • 66 (from top) Mirek Towski/DMI; Roger Karnbad/Celebrity Photo; Berliner Studio; Sam Mircovich/Reuters/Archive Photos • 67 (from top) Lisa Rose/JPI; Paul Fenton; Berliner Studio • 68 (from left) Mark J. Terrill/AP/WWP; Steve Granitz/Retna • 69 (from top) Steve Granitz/Retna; Richard Young/Rex Features; Kevoric Djansezian/AP/WWP; Lisa Rose/JPI • 70 (from left) Paul Smith/Feature Flash/Retna; Ron Davis/Shooting Star; Steve Granitz/Retna • 71 (clockwise from top) Paul Smith/Feature Flash/Retna; Mark J. Terril/AP/WWP; Ron Galella Ltd. • 72 (from top) Fitzroy Barrett/Globe Pictures; Paul Fenton/Shooting Star; Steve Granitz/Retna; Ruymen Newspapers/Ramey Photo Agency • 73 (from left) Ramey Photo Agency; Jeff Mitchell/Reuters/Archive (2); Rick Diamond/Image Direct • 74 (from top) Paul Smith/Feature Flash/Retna; Ron Davis/Shooting Star (2); Lisa Rose/JPI • 75 (clockwise from top) Eric Charbonneau/Berliner Studios; Kevin Mazur; Axelle/Bauer Griffin; Gregg DeGuire/London Features • 76-77 (clockwise from bottom left) Jeff Kravitz (4); Suzanne Plunkett/AP/WWP; Greg DeGuire/London Features; Jeff Kravitz/Film Magic; Kevin Mazur; Suzanne Plunkett/AP/WWP

SENSATIONS 78-79 Jill Connelly/Reuters/Corbis • 80 Mike Blake/Reuters/Corbis; (bottom) HBO • 81 Dorothy Low • 82 Neal Preston/Dreamworks; (bottom) Berliner Studios • 83 Kevin Mazur • 84 Erica Berger/Corbis Outline • 85 (top) Steve Friedman/Buena Vista; David Alloca/DMI • 86 Carlos Lopez-Barillas/Liaison Agency; Warner Bros. • 87 Dorothy Low; Nick Baratta/Teen People • 88 Bob Marshall/Universal Studios; (bottom) Phil Ramey • 89 Ann Summa/Liaison Agency • 90 Timothy Hursley; (inset) Eric Vanderville/Liaison Agency; (bottom) Tim Street-Porter/EMP • 91 Robert Beck/Sports Illustrated; (inset) Eric Risberg/AP/WWP • 92-93 Ken Regan/Camera 5 (2)

FAMILY MATTERS 94 Splash; (inset) AP/WWP • 95 (from top left) Peter Kramer/Galella Ltd.; Press Office Damiani/AP/WWP; CA Images; David Rohmer • 96-97 Nunn Syndication; (inset) PA Photos • 98 (clockwise from top left) Ramey Photo Agency; Phillip Gould for Denis Reggie; De Buissink/Rosenfeld & Associates/AP/WWP • 99 Backstreet Brides; (top) Mirek Towski/DMI; (bottom) Andre Csillag • 100 (from top) Lynne Cook; Cornell Weaver; Beth Hertzhaft • 101 (from top) Ron Galella; Kevin Mazur; Brenda Chase/Liaison Agency • 102-103 (clockwise from top left) Paul Schmulbach/Globe Photo; Annamaria Disanto/Online USA; Sylvain Gaboury/DMI; Olivia Barrionuevo/Globe Photos; Courtesy Jeffrey Asher; Phil Ramey • 104-105 (clockwise from top left) Brian Arias; Miranda Shen/Celebrity Photo; Richard Young/Rex; Vinnie Zuffante/Starfile; Gregg DeGuire/London Features • 106 (clockwise from top) Mark Sennet/Reflex; Julien Cornish Trestrail/PA; Kevin Mazur/AP/WWP • 107 (from left) Mike Powell/Allsport; Lawrence Schwartzwald/Liaison Agency • 108 Kyle Samperton/Women's Wear Daily • 109 (from top) Warner Bros.; Steven Granitz/Retna; Paul Smith/Retna • 110 (from left) Doug Loneman/Sipa; Henry McGee/Globe Photos • 111 (left) Evan Agostini/Liaison Agency; (top right) Ron Galella Ltd. • 112-113 (clockwise from top) Najlah Feanni/Saba; Times London/New International; Robin Platzer/Twin Images; Michael O'Neill; Jim Smeal/Galella Ltd.; Frank Trapper/Corbis Sygma

TRIBUTE 114-115 John Burgess/Santa Rosa Press Democrat/Liaison Agency • 116 (from top) Phil Wolcott Jr./Globe Photos; Hansel Mieth/CCP • 117 Everett Collection • 118 (from top) Neal Peters Collection; Peggy Sirota/Corbis Outline • 119 Anthony Neste/HBO • 120 Culver Pictures • 121 Kobal Collection • 122 Chris Ouellette/Corbis Outline • 123 (from top) Globe Photos; Lynn Goldsmith/Corbis • 124 Irving Newman/Archive • 125 Harry Borden/IPG/Matrix • 126 Peter Stackpole/Timepix • 127 (from top) Globe Photos; Everett Collection • 128 Kobal Collection • 129 (from top) Dean Dixon/Corbis; NBC/Globe Photos • 130 Bernard Gottfryd/Archive • 131 (from top) John Wilhelm; Stephen Rose; (inset) from *The Iron Tonic,* Harcourt, Inc • 132 Peter Stackpole/Timepix; NBC/Globe Photos • 133 Richard B. Levine • 134 Archive • 135 Gerardo Somoza/Corbis Outline • 136 Kevin Knight/Corbis Outline • 137 (from top) The Dallas Morning News/Corbis Sygma; AP/WWP • 139 EC Publications/AP/WWP (2) • 140 Corbis/Bettmann • 141 courtesy Universal Music